Why buy this book?

Carollyne Rayner has been an Alberta Marriage Commissioner for two years, coming naturally into this calling, with a broad background in adult education and motivation. An interested and involved Calgary resident for over 30 years, Carollyne is also a truly romantic spirit. In the course of her work she has met over 200 couples and discovered that most of you have the same questions. This book will help you answer those questions.

The ideal ceremony will reflect your own personalities. This book is intended to encourage you to write your own "I do," and to guide you through all the aspects of having a civil wedding. You will be encouraged to "write" your ceremony, to express your deeply emotional thoughts and feelings. As you follow the guidelines, you will find that fears about expressing yourself before an audience will decrease as you realize how rewarding it can be for you and your guests to have wedding vows that truly speak from your heart. When you write down the expectations you have, of the people who will support you in the ceremony, your big day can unfold smoothly, without omissions or unlooked-for surprises. Following an organized approach will help you to be sure that you have remembered all the details.

The book includes questions to ask when planning your wedding, information about legal requirements, historical background relating to some wedding traditions and rituals, numerous examples of wording for vows and special ceremonies, and sample readings that you can use.

You Can Write "I Do" and More. And there is "more" in this book. You can learn about having a Christening, or naming, for your child or about renewing your wedding vows in a civil ceremony with a marriage commissioner officiating. Sample ceremonies and checklists to guide you are included for these life passages as well.

Why are turtles on the cover of this book?

The author, Carollyne B. Rayner discovered many years ago that her spirit animal helper was the Turtle. Some people think of spirit animals as similar to guardian angels or guides. Others view them as divine forces or energies that we can call on when the need arises. Many believe seeing a turtle in its natural habitat or in a dream or other vision, may be a sign that your life is becoming too frenetic and that you need to slow down and to avoid the hubbub of the world around you for a time. Carollyne finds that the Turtle appears to her when she is trying to rush things, and urges her to persevere, to be patient, and to let things unfold in their due time.

The Turtle is a symbol that occurs in many cultures. It is the oldest of all the vertebrates and one of the most ancient reptiles. Turtles live in water, and their most unique feature is the sturdy shell, which serves as their home and affords them protection from virtually all predators. A turtle's metabolism is very slow and it moves as if it has plenty of time—and perhaps it does, since this creature's life span is equal to a human's. It is said that people who have the Turtle as their spirit helper are well-equipped to protect themselves and to provide shelter for themselves and their families. Many Native Americans see the Earth as a Turtle supporting human beings on her back. In some Eastern cultures, the shell of the Turtle is a symbol of heaven.

This book calls on the wisdom of the Turtle spirit to guide couples through the rituals associated with three of the most significant life passages they can experience.

Maruta Jacobs edited, designed, and typeset this book and her life has been filled with turtles. She married over twenty-five years ago, in a civil ceremony, to a man who chose to amuse their young children by drawing and colouring turtles for them. Her daughter has owned many turtles: live ones, ornamental ones, ones printed on t-shirts. Don't tell anyone, but she sometimes goes by the nickname, "Turtle."

Maruta has many interests and is a member of the Canmore Artists' and Artisans' Guild and of the Mountain Cabin Quilters' Guild (a reflection of her pursuit of fibre arts as well as editing and design work). She is the co-owner of Common Thread Design, located in Canmore, Alberta.

Debbie Chelan is the cover artist and has been able to visually express the life experiences of human beings, using Turtle spirit helpers as her guides. As a point of interest, the name Chelan, is very similar to the scientific name for the turtle, *chelonian*. Debbie works in watercolour, acrylic, and pastel media. She is a member of the Canmore Artists' and Artisans' Guild and the Federation of Canadian Artists. Chelan Art is based in Canmore and Kelowna.

Carollyne's small turtles, collected on her travels across Canada, the USA, the British Isles, France, Italy, Mexico, and Hawaii, remind her of the lessons to be learned from having patience and being well organized before taking action.

You Can Write
"I Do" and More
Wedding, Christening, and Renewal Ceremony

Carollyne B. Rayner

Turtle Publishing
Calgary, Alberta
Canada

First edition 2001 by Carollyne B. Rayner

Turtle Publishing
Box 63124
2604 Kensington Rd. N.W.
Calgary, Alberta T2N 4S5
Phone: (403) 283-4770
Fax: (403) 503-3356
Email: TurtlePublishing@shaw.ca
Website: www.craynerAlbertaMarriageCommissioner.com

National Library of Canada Cataloguing in Publication Data
Rayner, Carollyne B., 1944-
  You can write "I do" and more—

  Includes bibliographical references and index.
  ISBN 0-9689866-0-9

    1. Marriage service. 2. Baptism.
    I. Jacobs, Maruta A., 1954- II. Title.

BL619.M37R39 2001   392.5   C2001-911560-1

Printed and bound in Canada
Copyright 2001—Copyright registration 494573

This book is dedicated to my partner, George.

Without your love and support, George, none of this would have been possible.

You have always been available to listen to my ideas.

Acknowledgments

I would like to extend my special thanks to all those Brides and Grooms I have had the honour of working with to develop such loving and meaningful marriage ceremonies, to the Mothers and Fathers with children who wanted a special ceremony to introduce their wonderful new additions to friends and extended family, and to the experienced couples who have reconfirmed their love through a renewal ceremony with their family and friends. Without the feedback, encouragement and ideas you have given me, I would never have researched and completed this book.

Special thanks go to Maruta Jacobs, my editor, typesetter, book designer, coach and very good friend. Without your steady hand, and **stay-the-course** encouragement during the editing period, I would have given up the **race** long before we reached the finish line.

The following people have assisted with draft typing, technical computer support, and research. I would like to extend my sincere thanks to each of them for their ongoing support and valuable contributions in the completion of this book: George McKenzie, Heather-Ann Furseth, Paul Jacobs, Linda Sorensen, Judy Colborne, Susan Fleurant, Shawna Chong, William (Bill) Pisarcuk, Beryl Cahill, Edward Mueller, and Irene Ryckman.

For the use of their photographs, I wish to acknowledge: Bride and Groom — Mr. & Mrs. Tim & Jolyne Kalil; Renewal Couple — Mr. & Mrs. Bert & Heather Furseth: Baby's Christening Parents — Mr. & Mrs. Ben & Michelle Schofield with Baby Ethan Bentley.

Special thanks for the words of wisdom they have shared with both myself and the future readers of this book and my gratitude for reviewing portions of the draft manuscript go to: Nomi Whelan — Alberta Marriage Commissioner, Rick Kunelius — Alberta Marriage Commissioner (Banff); Laura Klotz — Alberta Marriage Commissioner (Hinton); photographer Colin Ferguson; and the Alberta Government Services — Vital Statistics, Alberta Registries Office. I am grateful to Brian Lee for his generosity in allowing me to quote from his book, *The Wedding M.C.* and to the Calgary and Canmore Public Library staff for research and forbearance beyond their job descriptions.

I owe a great debt to authors and poets, living and deceased, whose words have come to be included in the book. All efforts have been made to contact all those for whom contact information could be traced for permission to reproduce their words. However, much of the material included in the book has been collected over a long period of time and sources have become lost, so where our efforts have not been successful, thanks and apologies are extended to the authors. I hope that they would agree, "Do not inquire as to who said this, but pay attention to what is said." An invitation is extended to anyone, knowing where uncredited original authors can be contacted, to pass this information on to Turtle Publishing, so that they can be appropriately credited and acknowledged in subsequent editions of this book.

Last but not least I wish to extend my thanks to Debbie Chelan, the cover artist, for her beautiful interpretive art and for producing it in the midst of changing her own residence.

 Carollyne B. Rayner, marriage commissioner, author and publisher, has a background in adult education, public relations and marketing consulting. She is a life member of Beta Sigma Phi, Laureate Zeta Chapter, and Past Matron of Acacia Chapter #56, Order of the Eastern Star, in Calgary.

Carollyne was born and raised in Halifax, Nova Scotia. Her business career in training and marketing involved travel throughout the United States and all the Canadian provinces. She lived in Winnipeg and Vancouver before moving to Calgary in the early seventies and considers Alberta her home. When time permits, Carollyne enjoys golf. Her ideal vacation takes her to a warm ocean climate.

Contents

12 Contents

Civil Ceremonies: the Basics

And you thought a civil ceremony meant high-tailing it to Las Vegas or the office of the marriage commissioner! You could do either of those things, but more and more couples today are choosing to have secular ceremonies in traditional ways — inviting their nearest and dearest, not to a house of worship, but to a family member's home or another location that they find meaningful.

Under Alberta law, a couple can choose to be married at any location, of their choice, by an Alberta Marriage Commissioner. The Nikka Yuko Gardens in Lethbridge, the Wedding Pavillion in Calgary, the historical Deane House at Fort Calgary, and Jasper's Maligne Lookout are just some of the wonderful sites that couples have chosen. The only legal requirement is that the location you arrange must hold five people — the couple, two witnesses, and an Alberta Marriage Commissioner. So, be it a mountain meadow, your mom's backyard, a chapel, or a hot air balloon, you are entirely free to express yourselves when you marry with a marriage commissioner.

Why have a civil ceremony?

Couples who choose civil ceremonies usually fall into one of the following groups:

- They feel uncomfortable with the idea of a religious ceremony as neither person subscribes to an organized religion.
- Both bride and groom have a religion, but not the same beliefs.
- The couple's ideal ceremony is more creative than most — they may wish to have a particular reading by a friend, or to include Native American or other ethnic traditions, in the form of dance or song. Many clergy today are quite flexible, but this problem does arise.

Who can officiate?

Your officiant must be legally appointed to perform wedding ceremonies. In Alberta, this person is called an Alberta Marriage Commissioner. In the United States, this person is referred to as a Justice of the Peace and other jurisdictions may use their own terminology.

How does a civil ceremony differ from a religious one?

All civil ceremonies bypass traditions specific to a particular organized religion. A civil ceremony usually has the same basic exchange ("We are gathered here today ...") and other unity gestures (exchanges of vows, rings, or other symbolic gifts), a pronouncement ("I now pronounce you husband and wife"), kiss, and closing remarks as most church ceremonies.

You may want to eliminate the procession and recession (formal entrance and departure from the place where the ceremony occurs) or some other portion of the usual ceremonial sequence. In most cases, the bride and groom have greater input into the actual wording of their civil wedding ceremony than they would with a religious service. They can include special readings or musical selections, select or write personal vows, or have a short, sweet, very simple ceremony.

Alberta Marriage Laws

Alberta marriage ceremonies are valid throughout the world. Blood tests, residency requirements, and waiting periods are not required for marriages taking place in Alberta. Both the bride and groom must be 18 years old, or have written consent to the marriage from their own parent or legal guardian. If a couple's documentation is in order, it is possible to obtain a marriage license and to be married on the same day.

Before a marriage can take place, couples must obtain an Alberta Marriage License from a Registry Office in the Province of Alberta. This license is valid immediately and for three months from the date of issue.

To obtain a license, both the bride and groom must be present at the Registry Office and must each submit the following:

❧ Identification (driver's license, passport, or birth certificate)

❧ Father's full name and birthplace

❧ Mother's birth name, full name, and birthplace

❧ Final Divorce Decree if this will be a re-marriage

The license is turned over to the person who conducts the marriage ceremony. The couple receives a Civil Marriage Statement when the ceremony is completed. The marriage commissioner registers the marriage by submitting all signed

marriage documents to the Alberta Government Services
Registries, Vital Statistics Department in Edmonton, by mail,
after the ceremony. The information is then entered into the
Alberta Registries database. To obtain a copy of your Legal
Marriage Registration document, which is available in several
sizes and formats, the couple must contact an Alberta
Government Registry Agency, pay a fee, and complete all
necessary forms. To allow time for documents from the marriage
commissioner to be received and entered into the database, it is a
good idea to wait at least seven days after the marriage has taken
place to do this.

A marriage ceremony must be witnessed by two people, 18 years
of age or older. The marrying couple can supply their own
witnesses or request the Alberta Marriage Commissioner to
make the arrangements. Marriage ceremonies can also be
performed with the aid of an interpreter or assistant if the bride
or groom do not speak or understand English or have a disability
that makes communication difficult.

Rituals and Myths

Rituals and myths are two of the most powerful ways that societies encode and transmit important messages concerning social values. A ritual can be defined as: formal or ceremonial procedure, customary for religious or other solemn use.

The wedding ceremony, as used today, is a powerful ritual and has incorporated many associated customs over the centuries. Rituals, such as weddings, formalize the basis of most societies, the union of a man and a woman into a new state, that of a married couple. The ceremony acts out a symbolic joining of the families of the bride and groom into a supportive unit for the couple.

By providing a source of strength to a couple, their friends, and families, ultimately these types of rituals strengthen society as a whole.

As we enter a new century, we may feel we have replaced the value systems associated with traditional cultures with a plurality of competing value systems. Rituals and myths, the stories societies tell to support them, that were once central to all members of a particular society have lost their wide appeal.

However, pluralism does not lessen the need for rituals and myths. It underscores their importance. Some see modern western society as a battleground of competing rituals and myths, all struggling for recognition and power.

The messages contained in rituals and myths are so much a part of life that they are taken for granted. This is the source of their power. We can be so emotionally engaged in what is happening that we suspend disbelief and buy the messages. Effective advertising works the same way, with messages and values contained within media images. We are shaped by values we rarely recognize.

The stories we were told as young children often contained values that we retain as adults, perhaps partly because they were told within a family ritual and that ritual reinforced the myth. The ritual and the myth combined to reinforce the message. The message may be a set of values like "the importance of private property" as in *Goldilocks and the Three Bears.* "Who's been eating my porridge?" said the father bear. Or it may contain a strong moral (don't raise false alarms, you won't be believed when real trouble arises), as in *The Boy Who Cried Wolf.* In these instances, rituals and myths work together, powerful allies using the proven repetition technique of story, emotions, and imagination, blended in a communication that lasts.

Here is an example of a commonly recurring family ritual:

Father: "Get into bed and Daddy will tell you a story of Brer Rabbit. Which one would you like tonight?"

Child: "The one about the blackberry bush."

Father: "Ah yes, you like that one, don't you. OK. Ready?"
"Once upon a time Brer Rabbit was hopping happily along the road when he fell into one of Brer Fox's many traps..."

And so the story of how the rabbit outwits the fox — with a cunning deception — is recited once again, within the warm and loving environment of a parent and child preparing for bed. The weaker but cleverer rabbit escapes once again, from the bigger and stronger fox. The child will fall asleep learning a value of the culture — not to give up even though the odds may look overwhelming.

One reason why rituals and myths are such a powerful way to communicate value systems is because they employ two of the strongest and most lasting tools of communication — emotion and imagination.

Because rituals and myths are such excellent communicators of values, societies use rituals and myths to support laws and punishment systems. All societies enforce community rules with laws and provide punishments as deterrents.

Rituals and myths go much further. They don't just state what we should do or not do — they reinforce those messages with powerful appeals to emotions and sensibilities and they do it in a way that appeals to the imagination.

"Everyone knows" — ethics is as dry as dust and laws only challenge some people to break them. But tell a child a story about a puppet whose nose grows every time he tells a lie, repeat it a few times, and the message that lies have serious consequences is very likely to be absorbed into the life of that child.

Rituals express and pass on values, and although they may develop and evolve, this is a very slow process. People often practise family traditions that were dear to them when they were children, as well as developing new rituals of their own which may also be passed on.

Rituals and myths transmit some very old traditions. Weddings held during the Middle Ages were considered family and community affairs. The only thing needed to create a marriage was for both partners to state their consent to take one another as spouses. Witnesses were not always necessary, nor was the presence of the clergy. It wasn't official church policy, until the council of Trent in the 15th century ruled that a third party (a priest), as opposed to the couple themselves, was responsible for performing the wedding.

It was still later in the medieval period, before the wedding ceremony moved from the house of the bride, to the church. Festivities began with a procession to the church from the bride's home. Often, this was led by singing minstrels or pipers. The group often included a young man carrying a bride-cup of silver or silver-gilt and decorated with rosemary and ribbons. The bride walked next, attended by young men, knights or pages. Next in the procession were young girls carrying a bride cake and garlands of wheat. The bridegroom was led by two maidens and walked in the midst of his close friends, including the "best man." He was followed by various relatives, the invited, and uninvited, guests.

Vows were exchanged outside the church (the priest gave away the bride, not the father) and then everyone moved inside for mass. Afterward, invited guests and the rest of the procession returned to the bride's house for a feast.

Marriage is a ritual found in almost all cultures in the world. Weddings of the Renaissance and medieval period were similar, in content, to our civil and religious weddings today. In North America, weddings have moved from being mainly religious ceremonies; to become more relaxed, and often personalized, civil marriage ceremonies, with couples determining their vows and proceedings.

Couples often choose to follow various customs from the past. Some of these are included here with a short explanation on their origins.

The **bachelor dinner** may have originated in ancient Sparta, where a bridegroom always invited close friends to supper on the eve of his wedding. It is certain that the tradition is very old and was practised in many countries and at many times.

The **trousseau** has origins in the barter-price, purchase-price, and dowry systems. It was believed that a bride should come to her husband with various possessions so that he might be compensated, in advance, for his expenses in caring for the children that would follow.

Members of the **bridal party** can be viewed as a modern day evolution, which originated in "marriage by capture" times. Can you imagine the groom and his attendants as a raiding party venturing into enemy territory to carry off his chosen bride? Can you see the bride's attendants as her first line of "defense"?

Perhaps you prefer the image of the Saxon tradition, where the most senior of the bride's friends attended her for some days before the wedding, making the bridal wreath, preparing decorations for the wedding feast, and dressing the bride for the wedding itself.

The **white gown** served as a public statement, in Saxon times and through to the 18th century, that the bride brought nothing with her to the marriage and that her husband would not be held responsible for her debts.

The **veil** was introduced to Europe after the Crusades. It was not uncommon for the groom to bargain with the bride's father for her hand. She was swathed in a bridal veil and only revealed to her husband after the ceremony. In Saxon times, the bride's loose and flowing hair was her "veil." Wearing a wreath of orange blossoms on the veil, as a crown, was also introduced after the Crusades. Only the very wealthy could afford real orange blossoms, so artificial flowers and native flowers were also used. The Victorians developed a "language of flowers" where each type of flower had a different symbolic meaning which was very important in both courtship and marriage.

Wedding cakes have taken various forms at different times and places. The Romans broke a cake made of salted meal over the bride's head to symbolize abundance. In other early cultures, cakes were dropped on the bride's head and the pieces eaten by the guests for good luck. Early Britons baked large quantities of crackers which were placed in baskets for the ceremony and distributed to departing guests after the ceremony, to be taken home, to "dream on." During the Middle Ages, cakes were baked in various forms, referred to as "subtleties." The shape could be that of a castle or basket, reminiscent of our own traditional cakes, or of an animal. Sometimes, coins or silver charms were baked into the cake.

The **garter toss** seems to have originated in medieval times. It was then customary for guests to escort the newly-weds to their marriage bed, a situation that could get quite rowdy, especially if the guests were eager to help the couple undress. Therefore, the bride's garters were quickly removed and tossed to the mob as a distraction. The myth arose that faithfulness would result, if a man gave his love the garter of a bride.

Throwing rice or old shoes is another very old custom. Rice or grain symbolizes abundance, good luck, and fertility in many cultures. Among ancient Assyrians and Jews, the giving of a man's sandal symbolized good faith when a bargain was made. Among the Saxons, hurling a shoe indicated that authority had been passed from one man to another (presumably from the father to the new husband of the bride).

The **honeymoon**, in Northern Europe, was actually the month (moon) following the wedding during which the newly-married couple drank mead (a honey wine) so that their lives would be marked by sweetness.

Today we can include these and other customs in our marriage ceremonies. Plurality and diversity in culture allow each couple to chose to honour each other with rituals that will have meaning for them. This generation will write and adopt its own rituals and myths. I wish them well.

Planning Your Wedding

When you plan a wedding, it is important to ask yourself and your partner a number of questions to discover what is important to you. Of course, the most important questions relate to your relationship and whether you truly wish to marry each other. See the suggested readings section of this book if you wish to explore further in this area. Nomi Whalen's book *Before We Say "I Do"* is excellent for determining if your relationship has the basis for a lasting marriage.

In this chapter of *You Can Write "I Do,"* we will guide you in planning your wedding ceremony. Remember that when you have a civil marriage, there is no pre-wedding course or counselling session as a matter of course. If you would prefer to have such preparation for marriage, you will need to arrange for it separately. Some marriage commissioners offer this service, as do psychologists and family therapists.

Discuss with your partner:

 What is the most important thing we do together? How does this apply to our wedding ceremony?

If music is a central part of your lives, consider including a large musical component. If you enjoy rock climbing, do you want to marry on a cliff face or at the top after a climb? Is the smell of home-cooking and the coziness of a family setting what you crave most? Then consider getting married and having your reception at Mom's.

 Will it be a formal, informal, or very casual wedding? How do our families and friends fit into this plan? Will finding the right person to officiate at the wedding of our dreams be difficult?

 Who do we want to invite to our wedding?

 Would it be a good idea to have a wedding program to be handed out to our guests?

You can make use of a program to explain certain parts of the ceremony, list the participants and why you have asked them to be with you, tell what readings or music you have selected, or anything else you want your guests to be aware of. You can also print memorial information about people whom you are honouring. It is best to be brief enough that your guests can easily read the program while others are being seated. A program need not be expensive and you can print it yourself if you have a laser printer and some attractive paper, readily purchased at a stationery store. Or have the printer you are using for wedding stationery do the work.

 What style of vows do we wish to use in the ceremony? Do we prefer to say something quite traditional, or is modern verse or song more our style?

See the **Wedding Vows** section of the book to help yourselves decide. It is a good idea to start by reading the tried-and-true traditional vows. Certain phrases are legally required, so you will need to include those when you make your modifications. Use the **Marriage Ceremony and Vows** chapter as your guide to the legal requirements.

You will need to discuss what you plan to say with your officiant. Remember, you must to be comfortable with this person and he or she needs to be comfortable with you. Read aloud the vows you have written. What's on paper can come across quite differently when it is spoken, and short sentences are usually best. Even if your vows are brief, write them out and refer to them during the ceremony, or arrange to repeat after the officiant.

Will someone walk down the aisle with either or both of us? If yes, would we want it to be father, mother, both, a special friend or mentor, a beloved pet?

Who will our two witnesses be: best man and maid of honour, parents, adult children, both men, both women, one of each? Do we want them to participate actively in the ceremony, for example, by doing a reading? Do we just want them to stand with us?

Where will we stand during the ceremony?

Brides who stand to the left of groom are following a tradition that dates back to "marriage by capture" where the groom wore his sword on the right side (assuming he was right-handed) and needed his hand free to defend her against other suitors. Some churches prescribe where the bride and groom will stand. If you have a civil ceremony, you may choose to stand however you wish.

Do we wish to include any special candle ceremonies, such as the memorial candle ceremony, to remember a close family member or friend, or a unity candle ceremony? Who shall we ask to participate by lighting candles or doing a reading?

Please see the appropriate section of this book for more information about these ceremonies.

Will children participate in the ceremony? Will we formally present gifts to them? Who will help to guide young children through their roles and take charge of them when we are occupied with our own part in the formalities?

See later sections in this book for more information before you decide.

Will we present rings or other gifts, such as roses, to each other during the ceremony? What do we want included in the ceremony to explain this to our guests?

See the appropriate section in the book to help you plan more completely. If you have a program, consider including some information there.

Do we wish to include readings or performances by special friends?

There is a lot of room for personalizing your wedding in this area. Before you make a final decision, do some browsing at the library or in your favourite bookstore, listen to music together, even romantic movies can provide you with material to consider.

How will the signing of official documents (by the two of you, your witnesses and your officiant) be accomplished? Will we have a table in view of our guests or will we go to another room to do this?

After the signing, how do we want to be presented to the guests?

 Will we need to rehearse with all the participants in the ceremony?

In a rehearsal, no vows are spoken — the participants "walk" through their parts so that they will know where to stand, when to come "on," etc.

If you have answered these questions and any others that came to mind, you should be ready to choose your officiant. If you both belong to the same church, this question may have been answered already. If this is not the case, read on to the next chapter.

How to Choose
a Marriage Commissioner

If you have decided that a civil marriage ceremony best meets
your plans for your big day, you will need to decide on your
marriage commissioner. To find your ideal marriage commissioner,
interview the people recommended to you by friends, family, or
wedding consultants. See a complete list of Alberta Marriage
Commissioners at the Alberta government internet site listed in
the **Resources** section of this book.

You will need to ask a number of questions. Some can be readily
covered on the telephone, but a personal interview is a much more
desirable setting for many of the more detailed ones. We
recommend that you find answers to most of those listed below, to
be sure you are well prepared.

1. Are you available on the date we have chosen?

2. Will you meet with us for a personal interview so that we can decide if we wish to work with you? (Arrange this well before your chosen date.)

3. How long have you been performing marriages?

4. Why do you do this work?

5. Can you travel to the wedding site we have chosen?

6. Will there be an additional charge for travel? How much?

7. If we have not chosen a site, what recommendations can you make for a suitable site?

8. What do we need to do to get a marriage license?

9. When do we give you the marriage license?

10. Can you explain the difference between a "Civil Marriage Statement" and a "Marriage Registration Document"?

11. What happens to the papers that are signed after a marriage is performed?

12. What arrangements regarding the wedding will you make on our behalf and what do we need to arrange ourselves? Do you have any suggestions to make things work as smoothly as possible?

13. Do you have suggestions for our ceremony, sample vows you can show us?

14. How do you feel about performing a ceremony like the one we have planned?

15. How far in advance do we need to book your time for a rehearsal?

16. Is it appropriate to invite you (and your partner) to the rehearsal dinner and/or to the reception after the ceremony?

17. Would you give a blessing at the reception after the ceremony?

18. What is your fee for performing a marriage ceremony? Is a rehearsal included in the fee?

19. When do we pay you for your services? What type of payment do you accept?

Finally, assess how you feel about the marriage commissioner. Are you relaxed in his/her presence? Does he or she seem genuinely interested in you as a couple? Will your friends and family also feel that this is the right person to perform your ceremony? Do you think that the marriage commissioner feels empathy for you? Do you have a good feeling that the arrangements you have agreed on together will be performed to your satisfaction?

Bride & Groom
Mr. & Mrs. Tim & Jolyne Kalil
*But happy they, the happiest of their kind, whom gentle
stars unite; and in one fate their hearts, their fortunes,
and their beings blend!*
(James Thomson - 1748)

The Marriage Ceremony and Vows

When a marriage ceremony takes place, there are a number of legal requirements. Certain things must be said, using certain exact words. There is a great deal more that is discretionary, and can be decided by the couple if they choose to have a civil ceremony. In a religious ceremony, the traditions of the church will usually determine how the service is conducted, after the legal necessities have been satisfied.

If you are planning your own ceremony, you need to know very clearly what you must say and what you can write for yourselves to say. Here we have set out the framework of a sample ceremony, including the most common variations. At the beginning of each section, we have indicated whether it is optional, or required, that you say or do what follows. Where many options exist, you will be directed to the appropriate section of the book for more information.

Be aware also, especially if you are adding any special services to your ceremony, that you may need to ensure that certain things (flowers, candles, gifts and so forth) are in place before the start of the ceremony. The chapter, **Planning your Wedding,** and the chapters that relate to each special service, will help you ensure that you do not overlook these details.

Giving Away the Bride

This section is optional.
Marriage Commissioner: *Being assured that your love and your choice of each other, to be your lifelong companion, have your families' blessing, I ask, "Who gives this woman to be married to this man?"*

Reply [(a), (b), (c), or write your own words]**:** (a) *"I do."* (b) *"Her mother and I do."* (c) *"I do on behalf of her family and friends."* The father or special person may place the bride's hand in the groom's and then be seated.

Declaration of No Impediment to Marriage

Many couples believe that a wedding ceremony must include the question, "Is anyone present who objects to the marriage or knows of any reason why it should not take place?" Unless the marrying couple want the question to be included in the ceremony, there is no reason to do so, as Alberta law does not require it.

The bride and groom are required by Alberta law to speak the following exact words. Where "Bride" and "Groom" appear in bold italic type, the appropriate name is to be inserted.

Marriage Commissioner: *We welcome you on this special day to join together with ***Bride*** (insert name) *and* ***Groom*** (insert name) *as they celebrate their marriage.*

*Marriage is not to be entered into inadvisably or lightly but with discretion and reverence. ***Bride*** and ***Groom*** know that even as they look forward to their lives together and the happiness that their love can bring, it will require understanding, patience and forgiveness.*

With this understanding **Bride** *and* **Groom** *wish to be joined in marriage.*

Bride *and* **Groom,** *I call upon both of you in the presence of these witnesses to repeat after me*

Groom *repeat after me.* (The marriage commissioner speaks, and then the groom repeats, this section, line by line.)

"I do solemnly declare
that I do not know of any lawful impediment
why I, (insert full legal name of Groom),
may not be joined
in Matrimony to (insert full legal name of Bride).
I call upon those persons present
to witness that I, (insert full legal name of Groom),
do take thee, (insert full legal name of Bride),
to be my lawful wedded wife."

Bride, *repeat after me.* (The marriage commissioner speaks, and then the bride repeats, this section, line by line.)

"I do solemnly declare
that I do not know of any lawful impediment
why I, (insert full legal name of Bride),
may not be joined
in Matrimony to (insert full legal name of Groom).
I now call upon those persons present
to witness that I, (insert full legal name of Bride),
do take thee, (insert full legal name of Groom),
to be my lawful wedded husband."

Marriage Vows

Marriage vows are not mandatory and, according to the Alberta Marriage Act, do not have to be included in the ceremony if the couple do not wish to do so. It would be a very short ceremony, but a marriage would be legally complete with only the previous speeches by the bride and groom, followed by the marriage commissioner's statement that they are now married. Traditionally, couples make additional vows to give a feeling of completeness to the ceremony.

The vows, readings, and special ceremonies which follow are here for your information. Just one sample vow is included in this chapter, so that you may understand how the ceremony flows. For additional vows, refer to the chapter, **Wedding Vows**. In the following example, and in many other vows, the words are spoken by both the bride and groom. Each speaks in turn, to the other. The order in which marriage partners speak is a personal decision, as is the choice to speak the same or different vows. Substitute appropriate names wherever "Bride" and "Groom" appear in bold italic type.

Example of a Traditional Vow

Marriage Commissioner: ***Bride*** *and* ***Groom****, as an expression that your hearts are joined together in love, would you please join your hands.*

Groom*, do you take* ***Bride*** *to be your wedded wife, to live together in marriage? Do you promise to love her, comfort her, honour and keep her for better or worse, for richer or poorer, in sickness and health and forsaking all others, be faithful only to her?*

Groom: *I do.*

Marriage Commissioner: ***Bride***, *do you take* ***Groom*** *to be your wedded husband, to live together in marriage? Do you promise to love him, comfort him, honour and keep him for better or worse, for richer or poorer, in sickness and health and forsaking all others, be faithful only to him?*

Bride: *I do.*

Ring Vows

Rings are not a legal requirement. It is the couple's choice to use one, two, or no rings in their ceremony. The bride and groom may choose to write their own Ring Service. Select from the samples provided later in this book, or use the sample below.

Marriage Commissioner: *What Symbols do you offer to honour your Marriage?*

Reply: *We offer rings.*

Marriage Commissioner: *Traditionally, the marking of the passage to married status of husband and wife is honoured with the exchange of rings.*

These rings are a symbol of the unbroken circle of Love. Love freely given has no beginning and no end, no giver and no receiver for each is the giver and each is the receiver.

May these rings you are about to exchange, always remind you of the vows you have declared here today.

Groom, *you will place the ring on* ***Bride's*** *finger and repeat after me:*

*"****Bride***, *I give you this ring, as a symbol of my love and commitment to you."* (The groom repeats the statement.)

Bride, *you will place the ring on* **Groom's** *finger and repeat after me:*

*"***Groom***, I give you this ring, as a symbol of my love and commitment to you."* (The bride repeats the statement.)

Bride *and* **Groom**, *through the exchanging of these vows and rings you have pledged yourselves to sharing a common future.*

Special Services

The Special Services noted below are not legally required in any wedding ceremony, but they are options for your consideration. Your marriage commissioner should be able to provide you with suggestions if you chose to use any of these options. There is a separate chapter in this book, discussing each of the special services.

The bride and groom may choose from a variety of **candle ceremonies**. If used, candle ceremonies would be inserted at this point in a wedding ceremony.

The bride and groom may select the formal **Rose Ceremony** as their first gift to each other as a married couple. A modified version of this ceremony, included later in this book as the **Child's Gift Presentation Ceremony**, can be used to welcome children into a merged family unit.

Family or friends of the bride and groom can be requested to do a reading at this point in the ceremony in honour of the marriage. Please refer to the **Ceremony Readings** chapter for suggestions. Another popular option is to include one or more musical presentations.

Blessing and Declaration of Marriage

The marriage ceremony traditionally closes with a blessing and a declaration by the marriage commissioner that the bride and groom are now married.

Marriage Commissioner: *Bride and **Groom**, you have pledged yourselves to sharing a common future.*

As you stand on the threshold of your new life together – I offer this special blessing. (The Marriage Commissioner reads the blessing chosen by the couple. Please refer to the blessings section for inspiration.)

***Bride** and **Groom**, having witnessed your vows of marriage before your family and friends and upon the authority vested in me by the Province of Alberta, I announce with great joy that you are, from this time on, Husband and Wife.*

You may share your first kiss as a married couple!

At this point, the marriage documents must be signed by the couple, the officiant, and the witnesses. This is required by law. (The marriage commissioner arranges for delivery of this signed document, by mail, to the Alberta Government Services Registries, Vital Statistics office, in Edmonton, after the ceremony.)

The final presentation of the couple to those assembled is at their discretion and is not required.

Marriage Commissioner: *Ladies and gentlemen, I now present to you Mr. & Mrs.* _____ (you may elect to be called by your first names only).

Ceremony Summary

Basic ceremony	Full-service additions
	Welcome
	Bride is "given away"
	Marriage Commissioner
	asks if anyone objects
	to marriage
Couple, led by	
Marriage Commissioner,	
declare no impediment to marriage	
Couple, led by	
Marriage Commissioner,	
declare intent to marry	
	Vows are spoken
	Special services
	(ring, candle, gift ceremonies)
	performed
	Ceremony reading
	Blessing given
Marriage Commissioner	
states couple are married	
Documents signed	
	Newly married couple
	presented to guests

Wedding Vows

When your marriage is performed by an Alberta Marriage Commissioner, you have the option of writing your own unique wedding vows or making a selection from vows used previously by other couples. References to higher powers are made at your own discretion as there are no particular legal requirements.

Though many couples repeat identical vows (changing only the name of the person being addressed) there is no requirement to do that; the words spoken by the bride can differ from those spoken by the groom.

The vows printed below have been used during previous ceremonies. You are welcome to use them as they appear here or modify them to suit your own needs.

I come here today, _____, to join my life to yours, before this company. In their presence, I pledge to be true to you, to respect you, and to grow with you through the years. Time may pass, trials may come, no matter what we may encounter together, I vow to you today, that this love will be my only love. I will make my home in your heart from this day forward.

Today, I, _____,
*join my life to yours, not merely as your (**husband**/**wife**),*
*but as your friend, your lover and your confidant(**e**).*
Let me be the shoulder that you lean on,
the rock on which you rest,
the companion of your life.
With you, I will walk my path,
from this day forward.

As freely, _____,
as God has given me life, I join my life with yours.
Wherever you go, I will go;
whatever you face, I will face.
For good or ill, in happiness or sadness,
come riches or poverty,
*I take you as my (**husband**/**wife**),*
and will give myself to no other.

Where there has been cold, you have brought warmth;
where my life was dark, you have brought light.
_____, I pledge,
before this company,
*to be your (**husband**/**wife**) from this day forward.*
Let us make of our two lives, one life
and let us always honour and respect each other.

_____, *our miracle lies in the path*
we have chosen together.
I enter this marriage with you,
knowing that the true magic
of love is not to avoid change,
but to navigate it together successfully.
Let us commit to the miracle
of making each day work, together.
Whatever lies ahead, good or bad,
we will face together.
Distance may test us for a time,
and time may test us,
but if we look to each other first,
we will always see a friend.
_____, *look to me,*
for all the days to come;
*today, I take my place as your (**husband/wife**).*

*On this day, (**month**, **day**, **year**),*
I, _____, join myself to you,
*as your (**husband/wife**),*
before our family and friends.
May our days be long,
and seasoned with love,
understanding and respect.

I used to be afraid of falling in love,
of giving my heart away.
*How could I trust a (**man/woman**) to love me,*
*to give me all that I wanted to give to (**him/her**)?*
_____, when I met you,
I realized how much we could share.
You have renewed my life.
Today, I join that life with yours.

I came to this place today
*as a (**man/woman**) standing alone,*
I will walk from it by your side.
Today, I cross the threshold with you
and enter into a lifetime commitment.
_____, I commit myself to you
*as your (**husband/wife**).*

_____, I love you
and on this day I wed you.
Not just for who you are,
but for who I am when I am with you.
I love you not only for what you've done with your life,
but also for what you're doing with mine.

I love you for making me happy and whole,
because that is what you do, _____,
without a doubt, just by being yourself.
Such a simple thing,
but no one else in the world can do it, only you forever!
This day, before our family and friends,
with joy in my heart,
*I pledge myself to you as your (**husband**/**wife**),*
promising to love you
and to cherish our moments together,
for now, and forever!

_____ , I take you,
*to be my lawfully wedded (**husband**/**wife**).*
Before these witnesses,
I vow to love you
and care for you as long as we both shall live.
I take you, with all your faults and your strengths,
as I offer myself to you, with my faults and strengths.
I will help you when you need help
and I will turn to you when I need help.
I choose you as the person with whom I will spend my life.

_____, you are my greatest love
and my last love.
Until I met you
I didn't give true love much thought,
but since you came into my life,
I constantly search to find the words
to tell you how much I love you
— how I adore you.

It is difficult for me
to verbalize my feelings for you,
because mere words can't begin
to express my deep love.
I thank God for you, _____,
and I pledge myself to you now,
to be your ever-faithful **husband/wife**.
I give you my mind,
my body, and I promise
to love you and cherish you
for as long as we both shall live.

Union of Love

These words are spoken in unison by the couple. They should face each other as they do so.

We will forever love one another

and share our most intimate thoughts,

promise to hold

and cherish and

value each other.

We will live each day,

as if our last,

vowing never to go to bed angry.

If sorrow enters our lives,

we pledge to one another

that together we will

see things through.

As we grow old and

we slowly begin to change –

we will look into each other's eyes

and know that what we have

will never die.

Personalized Vows

These vows are meant to be spoken directly to the partner and the partner's child/children. The speaker should face each person and may take their hands when addressing them.

(**Bride/Groom**'s name), *I choose you,*

(**Child**'s name, if more than one, list all in turn),

and you, (**Bride/Groom**'s name),

to be my family.

I promise to honour and respect you **both/all**,

and to provide for you,

to the best of my ability.

I promise to make our home a haven

where trust and love and laughter are abundant.

I make these promises

lovingly and freely

and vow to honour them

all the days of my life.

Children's Family Vow

If the parents joining in marriage have a child/children whom they are bringing into the newly created family, they may wish to use the following as a special reading before reciting their personal vows to each other.

To marry the person
you have set your heart upon is a joy,
unparalled in human life.

I, _____,
choose you, _____,
as my life partner,
*along with (**child/children**'s name(s) _____),*
whom I have been honoured
to love and share as family.

Together we will build a loving future.
I offer my strength and support.
I offer my faith and trust in you.
I offer my friendship and understanding,
to have a lifetime, together,
filled with joy and love.

Different Vows for Groom and Bride

It is not required that the bride and groom speak the same vows. The couple should feel free to write the words that each would like to say to the other. Just as their personalities differ, their words may also differ, if that is their choice.

They may speak in any order they desire. In this example, the groom speaks first.

_____, *I bring myself,*
to you this day,
in the presence of our families,
friends and nature
to share my life with you.
May my unconditional
and endless love for you,
create a beautiful place,
where all your hopes and dreams,
of marriage will grow.
I vow to be there for you,
faithfully, and always.
I will strive to bring love,
unity, peace and grace to our home,
providing a firm foundation,
for everything that we will build together,
as your husband from this day forward.

The bride replies to the groom's vow.

I come here today, _____,
before our families and friends,
and in their presence,
I pledge to be true to you,
to respect you,
and to grow with you.
Time may pass,
fortune may smile,
and trials may come.
No matter what we encounter together,
I vow that this love will be my only love.
I will make my home in your heart,
as your wife from this day forward.

Ring Ceremonies

The traditions regarding the giving of rings vary. In Canada and the United States, it is usual for both husband and wife to wear a ring as a symbol of marriage. The rings can have the same or different designs. Occasionally, only the woman will wear a ring and the reasons for this are probably as numerous as the marrying couples making this choice.

Rings in many European countries are worn on the third finger of the right hand, not on the left hand as they are here. Other cultures employ other types of jewellery to symbolize the married state or no jewellery at all.

There are no legal requirements in this matter and couples should feel free to make whatever choices they find meaningful, whether they honour a family tradition or blaze their own trail.

The Blessing of the Rings

This blessing, if you choose to use it, takes place before the giving of ring(s) occurs.

Marriage Commissioner: *These rings are a symbol of the unbroken circle of Love. Love freely given has no beginning and no end, no giver, and no receiver, for each is the giver and each is the receiver. May these rings you are about to exchange, always remind you of the vows you declare today.*

In a two-ring ceremony, the groom places his ring on the bride's ring finger, and the bride in turn, places her ring on the groom's ring finger. The ring vows are then spoken by each, in turn, to the other. Where bold italic text appears in the vow, names or correct designations should be inserted.

Sample Ring Vows

Bride/Groom: *Love has given us wings,*
and our journey begins today.
Bride/Groom, *wherever the wind may carry me,*
*I will stay by your side as your **husband/wife**.*
Take this ring as a sign of my love.

Bride/Groom: ***Bride/Groom***,
with free and unconstrained soul,
I give you all I am and all I am to become.
Take this ring, and with it my promise of faith,
patience, and love for the rest of my life.

Bride/Groom: *What have I to give you, **Bride/Groom**?*
The promise to take you as my only love from this day forward,
to stand by your side, to listen when you speak,
to comfort you when you cry,
and to join your
laughter with my own.
*Take this ring, and be my **husband/wife**.*

Bride/Groom: *Bride/Groom,*
I bring this ring,
shaped in the symbol of completeness and eternity,
and I give it to you to wear
so that we will always remember our marriage vows.

Bride/Groom: *To marry the person*
you have set your heart upon
is a joy unparalleled in human life.
Bride/Groom*, take this ring*
as a sign of my faith and
my commitment to our love
and share this joy with me today.

Bride/Groom: *Two flames, one light.*
Bride/Groom*,*
I offer you this ring as a sign of life,
and myself as your **husband/wife***.*
Let us always walk toward the light.

Bride/Groom: *In pledge of the vow of marriage*
made between us,
I offer you this ring, **Bride/Groom***.*
I love you so much
and I am proud to be your **husband/wife***.*

Bride/Groom: *Today we have moved from*
*"I" to "We," **Bride/Groom**.*
Take this ring as a symbol of my decision
to join my life with yours until death should part us.
I walked to this place to meet you today;
we shall walk from it together.

Bride/Groom: *Just as this circle is without end,*
my love for you is eternal.
As it is made of gold substance,
my commitment to you will never fail.
*With this ring, **Groom/Bride**, I thee wed.*

Bride/Groom: ***Bride/Groom**,*
it is my gift to you,
to be your best friend,
to respect, to support you, and to share my life with you,
throughout the years to come.
With this ring I pledge my commitment.

Bride/Groom: ***Bride/Groom**, I pledge to you*
with all my heart and being,
to love and support you in all ways.
With this ring I pledge my love and commitment,
forever and ever.

Bride/Groom: ***Bride/Groom***, *take this ring,*
and remember that today
I give myself to you.
Accept what I have given
and treasure it always, for it is
a gift of the heart.

Bride/Groom: ***Bride/Groom***, *I give you this ring*
as a symbol of my wedding vow,
and with all that I am,
and all that I have, I honour you.
With this ring I thee wed.

Memorial Candle Ceremony

If the couple wishes, departed family members can be remembered through a special memorial candle lighting ceremony. Memorial candles can be lit (by the mothers of both the bride and groom or by another selected family member) before the wedding ceremony begins.

If the family desires, the marriage commissioner will announce the names of the family members that are being remembered. The couple may choose anyone they wish to read the verse below (inserting names or appropriate pronouns as needed) or any other of their choosing.

Memorial Candle Verse

We wish _____, the family member(**s**) we have lost,

Could be with us today,

Because **he/she/they** were like our Earth and Sky

Before **he/she/they** went away!

We light these candles so that we might

Bring **him/her/them** here a while,

As we remember **his/her/their** bright flame,

His/Her/Their laughter and **his/her/their** smiles!

We wish that **he/she/they** could feel with us

The happiness we feel,

Because knowing that **he/she/they** knew our joy

Would make it all more real!

But even though **he/she/they is/are** not with us

His/Her/Their presence is still strong

Because in **his/her/their** heart(**s**) we'll always find

The love for which we long!

The Unity Candle Ceremony

A Unity Candle Ceremony is not a legal requirement. It is a service that any bride and groom can include in their wedding ceremony. A number of variations are possible when lighting the candles. Guests, children, and the couple themselves can play a role in lighting candles.

Usually two tapers and a large "unity" candle are used, but variations that honour deceased family members (see **Memorial Candle Ceremony**) or anything else that has significance for the bride and groom can also be employed. Mothers, grandparents, or friends may be chosen to light the taper candles prior to the start of the ceremony.

Please make safety considerations a critical part of your planning when you choose to have a candle ceremony.

This checklist contains points to consider in preparing for a unity candle ceremony.

1. Obtain permission for the use of lighted candles at the location where your wedding ceremony will take place.

2. Determine how the space can be used to the best advantage. For example, where will guests sit? Where will you enter? Where will the candles be located so that they are safe and visible during the ceremony?

3. Select a small sturdy table on which to place the two tapers and the unity candle. Decide whether you want flowers or some greencry at the base of your candles or perhaps in a vase, which would also sit on this table.

4. Determine if you will also use this table when you sign the register, or only during the candle ceremony.

5. Determine if you will require one or more chairs for signing the marriage register and related documents. Decide whether a tablecloth will be used to cover this table.

6. Purchase two dripless taper candles to fit your own or the location's candleholders.

7. Purchase a suitable dripless "Unity Candle" and candleholder, if needed.

8. Light the candlewicks for a moment, before the ceremony, so they will be easier to light during the ceremony.

9. Review who will light the tapers. (Refer to suggestions given in the sample ceremonies on the following pages.)

Some couples believe that leaving the individual taper candles lit after the lighting of the unity candle symbolizes individuality within the commitment of marriage. Others believe that extinguishing them shows their devotion to one another. Whether you extinguish the candles is a personal decision and, like many aspects of wedding planning, is up to you.

If you choose to extinguish your tapers, you may wish to use this reading:

Marriage Commissioner: *As **Bride** and **Groom**,*
together light the centre Unity Candle,
they will extinguish their own candles,
thus letting the centre candle
symbolize the union of their lives.
As this one light cannot be divided,
neither can their lives together be divided.

🕯

If you prefer to leave your tapers lit, this reading is an option:

Marriage Commissioner: *As **Bride** and **Groom***
came into their marriage relationship
as individuals, they do not lose their identity,
rather they have their individuality
to support and strengthen the relationship of marriage.
Therefore, the three candles remain lit,
one for each of them,
and one for their marriage,
as symbols of their commitment
to each other and
to a lasting and loving marriage.

The following examples of candle ceremonies are offered as suggestions. You may select standard verses, or mix and match the words to best suit your personal lifestyle.

Unity candle ceremony if children are involved

The two tapers should already be lit when this ceremony begins. Adult children, other relatives, or family friends can perform this service for the marrying couple.

Marriage Commissioner: *Bride and **Groom**,*
two lighted candles symbolize your separate lives,
your separate families and your separate sets of friends.

I ask each of you to take one candle and then,
together, to light the centre Unity Candle.
The individual candles represent
your individual lives before today.
Lighting the Unity Candle in the centre
represents the joining of your two lives into one light,
and represents the joining together
of your two families and sets of friends to one.

The lighting of the centre candle represents
not only the union
*of **Bride** and **Groom**, in marriage,*
but the unity formed in this new family.
Your lives will now shine as one family.

🕯

Unity candle
ceremony where all candles remain lit

Prior to the start of the wedding ceremony, the two tapers should be lit by persons especially selected, by the bride and groom, to do so. The bride and groom light the unity candle, together, when the marriage commissioner requests during the ceremony.

Marriage Commissioner: *This marriage*
is only the start of a lifetime of sharing.
The love in your hearts,
the candles standing lit on this table, symbolize
the individuality of **Bride** *and* **Groom,**
as they use the flames to light the Unity Candle.
The individual flames do not extinguish
even though the flame of the union candle burns brightly.
As you stand on the threshold of a new marriage,
respect each other's individual rights
and you will flourish in the happiness of your marriage.
As you walk hand in hand,
heart by heart,
through all the days of your lives,
may the blessings of life,
the value of family and friends,
and the joy of love be your constant companions.

🕯

Unity candle
ceremony where candelabra(s) are used

Some wedding locations, such as the Wedding Pavillion in Calgary, have large formal candelabra at the site. At these locations, the candles would already be lit when guests begin to enter and would remain lit throughout the ceremony.

If the bride or the groom is unable to reach a tall candelabra, a small pre-lit votive candle can be placed on the signing table or other convenient location so that the flame can be used to light the tapers at the appropriate time in the wedding ceremony.

Marriage Commissioner: *Bride and **Groom**,*
this marriage is only the start of a lifetime
of sharing the love in your hearts.
The two lighted candelabra standing in the room
symbolize your separate lives,
your separate families,
and your separate sets of friends.

I ask that you each take a candle
and using the flames from the candelabra
light the Unity Candle resting on this table.

The lighting of the centre candle represents
*not only the union of **Bride** and **Groom** in marriage,*
but the unity formed,
in which all your lives will now shine
as part of this extended family.

🕯

Unity candle
ceremony with guests lighting candles

Some locations, which do permit other types of candle ceremonies, might not permit this one, due to insurance issues relating to fire safety. This kind of ceremony could work well for a wedding being held in an outdoor, sheltered setting.

Please be aware of safety concerns at all times when using candles. In an outdoor setting, be prepared to change plans if weather conditions, such as a windy day, would make candle-lighting unsafe.

This unity ceremony allows for audience participation. Candle lighting originates at the back of the room, or outdoor area, with lights being passed from candle to candle through the ranks of the guests. A designated member(s) of the wedding party then lights the candelabra (if used) and the tapers representing the bride and groom.

If passing of candle flames is not permitted at the chosen wedding site, it may be possible to use a variation of the previous candelabra ceremony.

The candelabra candles would be lit at the beginning of the wedding ceremony by a chosen individual (perhaps mothers of the bride and groom or other persons chosen by them). Then, when this point in the service arrived, designated individuals would come forward to light the tapers from the candelabra flames (either directly or by using the pre-lit votive candles as above).

Marriage Commissioner: *Bride and **Groom**,*
this marriage is only the start
of a lifetime of sharing
the love in your hearts.
The two candles standing lit on this
table symbolize your separate lives,
your separate families,
and your separate sets of friends.

***Bride** and **Groom**, will you each take a candle*
and using its flame,
light the Unity Candle
resting on this table.

The Unity Candle symbolizes your two lives,
which are now joined as one light,
and represents the joining of your two families
and sets of friends into one.
Notice that the individual flames are not extinguished,
even as the flame of the union burns brightly.
Respect each other's families and your own individual rights
and you will flourish in the happiness of your Marriage.

May the blessings of life,
the value of your family and friends,
and the joy of love be your constant companions.

The Rose Ceremony

Couples choosing to incorporate a rose ceremony in their marriage ceremony are recognizing that the rose is considered a symbol of love. To many, a single rose symbolizes one thing — the words "I love you."

The symbolism of the rose is formalized in a ritual where the couple give each other a gift of a rose on their wedding day and promise each other that they will continue to use this very powerful symbolism in their future life together. For example, they may wish to tend a rose garden together, choosing its location and jointly participating in caring for it. They may agree on a special location within their home, where each could leave a gift of a rose for the other, to communicate deep feelings that might be difficult to put into words at particular time. The exact way that rose symbolism will be used can be as individual as the couples themselves.

When a rose ceremony will be part of the marriage ritual, the couple will need to agree on their plans for using rose symbolism in their lives, whether the rose is to be an annual gift to represent a renewal of vows, a way to communicate without words, or some other option of their own choice. The marriage commissioner should then be asked to explain the symbolism to the wedding guests or to lead the couple in speaking of the symbolism to each other as they exchange the gift of a single rose.

The following is an example of how such a ceremony might be conducted. Substitute names as needed wherever "bride" and "groom" appear in bold type.

Marriage Commissioner: *The Rose Ceremony recognizes your new and most honorable titles, "Husband and Wife." You have given each other, today, on your wedding day your first gifts, your wedding rings – which shall always be an outward demonstration of your vows of love and respect, and a public display of your commitment to each other.*

As a man and a woman you exchanged rings, and now, entitled to be called "husband" and "wife," it is fitting that your first gifts to each other, as husband and wife, will be gifts of a single rose.

Bride *and* **Groom***, wherever you make your home now, or in the future; I ask that you both pick one very special location for roses. On each anniversary of this truly wonderful occasion, I say to you that you should both take a rose to that spot – as a recommitment to your marriage – and as a recommitment that yours will be a marriage based upon love.*

Bride *and* **Groom***, please exchange your first gifts as husband and wife.* (At this point the couple, each of whom has been holding a single rose, exchange their roses.) *In some ways, it seems like you have not done anything at all. Just a moment ago you were each holding one small rose – and now you are each holding one small rose. In some ways a marriage is like this. In some ways, tomorrow is going to seem no different than yesterday. But in fact, today, just now, you both have given and received one of the most valuable and precious gifts in life – one I hope you always remember – the gift of true and abiding love, freely given within the devotion of marriage.*

In every marriage, there are times where it is difficult to find the right words. It is easiest to hurt those whom we most love. It is easy to be hurt by those whom we love. It might be difficult sometimes, in words, to say "I am sorry," "I forgive you," " I need you," or "I am hurting." If this should happen, if you simply cannot find the right words, leave a rose at that spot which you have both selected for a rose. It will say for you what matters most to you and should overpower all other things and all other words. That rose will say the words: "I still love you." Your partner should accept your rose, in place of the words that you cannot find, and remember the love and hope that you both shared here today.

Bride *and* **Groom***, if there is anything you remember of this marriage ceremony, it should be that it was love that brought you here today, it is only love which can make yours a glorious union, and it is by love that your marriage shall endure.*

Child's
Gift Presentation Ceremony

If either the bride or groom has a child or children, they may wish to consider including a child's gift presentation in their ceremony. This kind of presentation often feels very welcoming, especially to younger children. The gift chosen should have lasting value. Many parents like to give a gift that can be worn by the child, for example, a pin or pendant.

The gift presentation can be made before the couple exchange their own vows or afterwards. Someone should be appointed to assist with young child/children during the presentation ceremony. If the parent's new partner will be assisting at the presentation, choose another friend or relative to help the child/children when he/she/they are called to the front and when they rejoin the seated guests.

The marriage commissioner speaks as shown in the example below or as otherwise arranged. The parent or couple speaks as directed by the marriage commissioner. Where bold italic type appears the name or other appropriate description of the person is inserted into the text.

To assist the parent of the child/children, the marriage partner may wish to have the gift(s) in his/her pocket or other convenient place, ready for the presentation.

Marriage Commissioner: *It is my honour to be a part of this special presentation to the* **Child/Children** *of* **Parent** *at the time of* **his/her** *marriage.*

Would **Child/Children** *come to the front, please!* (The parent or couple greet(s) the child/children.)

Parent (or couple together) *will say the following:* **Child**, *as a sign of our love, now and forever,* **I/we** *offer you this gift as a permanent reminder of the love we all share as a new family today.* (The parent of the child gives the chosen gift to the child to wear or hold, as appropriate, assisted by their partner. If there is more than one child, this is repeated for each child in the family.)

Child/children, *you may return to your seat(s) for the remainder of the wedding ceremony.*

Ceremony Readings

Ceremony readings may be done by anyone of the couple's choosing, such as the marriage commissioner, a family member, or a friend. There are many sources of readings, and couples often find that a visit to the library is useful. The length of the reading and its content is according to your own choice. In this section of the book you will find a variety of readings used in wedding ceremonies previously to give you a starting point in your search to find the perfect reading for your ceremony.

May this man and this woman be a blessing and a comfort to each other.

May they share their dreams, console each other in sorrows, and help each other in all of life's challenges.

May they encourage each other in whatever they set out to achieve.

May they trust each other, trust life, and be unafraid.

May they love each other and offer love and support to those around them.

May your marriage bring you all of the excitement a marriage should bring.

And may life grant you patience, tolerance, and understanding for each other.

Marriage is not only a commitment between two lovers, it is also an agreement between two friends.

Allow each other time to be an individual, respect each other's wishes as well as each other's dreams.

Bride and Groom, nothing is easier than saying words and nothing is harder than living them, day after day after day.

What you promise today, must be renewed and decided again tomorrow, and the tomorrow after that, and the tomorrow after that one.

Concern for each other

It should never be said of either of you,

that you show more concern for a friend than you do for each
other.

More kindness, gentleness, and concern

needs to be shown in the privacy of your own home

than anywhere else.

Indeed, your home should be a haven from all the

confusion and craziness the world will create.

Faithfulness to each other, in every way,

is the primary ingredient that will keep all those

above-mentioned virtues in order

and produce the joy you seek at this joining ceremony.

Hallmarks of True Love
Newell W. Edson

1. A genuine interest in the other person and all that he or she says or does.

2. A community of tastes, ideals, and standards with no serious clashes.

3. A greater happiness in being with the one person than with any other.

4. A real unhappiness when the other person is absent.

5. A great feeling of comradeship.

6. A willingness to give and take.

7. A pride in the other person when comparisons are made.

Overheard at a Cowboy's Wedding

Judy A. Barnes

As you begin your wedded life,
Joined together
As husband and wife,
Pull together as a matched team,
Neither going to the extreme.

Lasso kindness and hold her tight,
Never let love out of your sight.
Now hitched for a lifetime project,
For one another show respect.

Saddle up for the blissful ride,
Corral some humor on the side. (You'll need it!)
Don your hats and pull on your boots,
Parson pronounced you in cahoots,
As you walk towards the western skies,
At all costs, avoid the cow pies.

Cherokee Prayer

God in heaven above, please protect the ones we love.

We honour all you have created as we pledge our hearts and lives together.

We honour Mother Earth, and ask for our marriage to be abundant and to grow stronger through the seasons.

We honour fire, and ask that our union be warm and glowing, with love in our hearts.

We honour wind, and ask that we sail though life safe and calm as in our father's arms.

We honour water to clean and soothe our relationship, that it may never thirst for love.

With all the forces of the universe you have created, we pray for harmony and true happiness, as we forever grow young, together.

A Spiritual Reading

(This reading is based on the Cherokee Prayer.)

We stand before all creation as **Bride** and **Groom** pledge their hearts and lives together.

We honour earth – and wish your marriage to grow stronger through the seasons. We honour fire – and wish your union to be warm and glowing with love in your hearts. We honour wind – and wish that you sail through life safe and calm. We honour water – to cleanse and soothe your relationship – that it may never thirst for love. With all the forces of the universe, we ask for harmony and true happiness, as you forever grow young, together.

Bride and **Groom**, in your journey, you will search in all directions for guidance. Look to the West for the mountains. This will give you strength to overcome life's obstacles. Look to the North for the star that never moves. This will give you direction. May you see it for many years. Look to the East for the light of the sun. May it shine happiness upon you always. Look to the South for warmth. May the warm winds of the South bring you the comforts of home.

It was these forces that brought you together, and they will help to guide you and keep your love fresh, alive and growing into the future.

Kahlil Gibran on Marriage

Then Almitra spoke again and said, And what of Marriage, master?

And he answered saying:

You were born together, and together you shall be forevermore.

You shall be together when the white wings of death scatter your days.

Ay, you shall be together even in the silent memory of God.

But let there be spaces in your togetherness,

And let the winds of the heavens dance between you.

Love one another, but make not a bond of love:

Let it rather be a moving sea between the shores of your souls.

Fill each other's cup but drink not from one cup.

Give one another of your bread but eat not from the same loaf.

Sing and dance together and be joyous, but let each one of you be alone,

Even as the strings of a lute are alone though they quiver with the same music.

Give your hearts, but not into each other's keeping.

For only the hand of Life can contain your hearts.

And stand together yet not too near together:

For the pillars of the temple stand apart,

And the oak tree and the cypress grow not in each other's shadow.

Serenity Reading

I would like at this time, to speak of some of the things which many of us wish for the both of you. We wish for you a home, not just a place of stone and wood, but an island of peace, a place from which you will receive strength and support that stays and carries you throughout your daily lives. We hope that your home encompasses the beauty of nature, that it has within it the elements of simplicity, beauty, silence, and colour, in accord with your dreams and aspirations.

Bride and **Groom**, you are about to make promises to one another. Today, these vows are beautiful words representing even more beautiful intentions. But you will find that as you live these vows over the years, investing your time, your love, and your commitment to one another, the happy times of your life will be twice as joyous, because there will be someone to share those joys with. And when life gets tough, it will only be half as bad, because there will be someone by your side to help carry the burden.

For those times when life presents all of us with challenges, I would like to offer you the serenity prayer to remember: "God grant me the serenity to accept the things that I cannot change, the courage to change the things I can, and the wisdom to know the difference."

Friendship

It is often said that it is love that makes the world go round. However, without a doubt, it is friendship, which keeps our spinning existence on an even keel.

True friendship provides so many of the essentials for a happy life. It is a foundation on which to build an enduring relationship. It is a mortar to bind us together in harmony. And it is the calm, warm protection we sometimes need when the world outside seems cold and chaotic.

True friendship holds up a mirror to our foibles and failings, without destroying our sense of worthiness. True friendship nurtures our hopes, supports us in our disappointments, and encourages us to grow to our best potential.

Bride and **Groom** came together as friends. Today, they pledge to each other not only their love, but also the strength, warmth, and, most importantly, the fun of true friendship.

Love Is

Susan Polis Schutz

Love Is
Being honest with yourself at all times,
Telling, listening, respecting the truth
And never pretending,
Love is the source of reality.

Love Is
An understanding that is so complete
That you feel as if you are
A part of the other person,
Accepting the person just the way they
Are and not trying to change them
To be something else.
Love is the source of unity.

Love Is
The freedom to pursue
Your own desires
While sharing your experience
With the other person,
The growth of one individual

Along side of, and together with,
The growth of another individual.
Love is the source of success.

Love Is
Giving and taking in a daily situation,
Being patient with
Each other's needs and desires.
Love is the source of sharing.

Love Is
Knowing that the other person
Will always be with you
Regardless of what happens,
Missing the other person
When they are away,
But remaining near in heart
At all times.

Love is the source of security.
Love is "the source of Life."

Kahlil Gibran from *The Prophet*,
passages from on Marriage and on Love

"Love one another, but make not a bond of that love:
Let it rather be a moving sea between the shores of
your souls."

"And stand together, and yet not too near together:
For even the pillars of the temple must stand apart,
And the oak tree and the cypress will not grow
in each other's shadow."

Remember that
"Love gives naught but itself and takes naught but from
 itself. Love possesses not, nor would it be possessed;
For love is sufficient unto love."

"And think not you can direct the course of love,
for love, if it finds you worthy, directs your course."

How Do I Love Thee?
Elizabeth Barrett Browning
"Sonnets from the Portuguese"

How do I love thee? Let me count the ways.
I love thee to the depth and breadth and height
My soul can reach, when feeling out of sight
For the ends of Being and ideal Grace.
I love thee to the level of every day's
Most quiet need, by sun and candle-light.
I love thee freely, as men strive for right;
I love thee purely, as they turn from praise.
I love thee with the passion put to use
In my old griefs, and with my childhood's faith.
I love thee with a love I seemed to lose
With my lost saints - I love thee with the breath,
Smiles, tears, of all my life! - and, if God choose,
I shall but love thee better after death.

I Wish You Love
Author unknown

I do not wish you joy without a sorrow,
Nor endless day without the healing dark,
Nor brilliant sun without the restful shadow,
Nor tides that never turn against your back.
I wish you love, and strength, and wisdom,
And gold enough to help some needy one,
I wish you songs, but also blessed silence,
And God's sweet peace when every day is done.

Celebration of Marriage

Marriage is a supreme sharing of experience and an adventure in the most intimate of human relationships. It is the joyous union of two people whose comradeship and mutual understanding have flowered in romance. Today, **Bride** and **Groom** proclaim their love and commitment to the world, as we gather here, at the start of the new life they now undertake together.

The joy we feel now is a solemn joy, because the act of marriage has many consequences, both social and personal. Marriage requires "love," a word we often use with vagueness and sentimentality. We may assume that love is some rare and mystical event, when in fact it is our natural state of being.

So what do we mean by "love"? When we love, we see things other people do not see. We see beneath the surface, to the qualities that make our beloved special and unique. To see with loving eyes, is to know inner beauty. And to be loved is to be seen, and known, as we are known to no other. One who loves us, gives us a unique gift: a piece of ourselves, but a piece that only they could give us.

We, who love, can look at each other's life and say, "I touched his life," or "I touched her life," just as an artist might say, " I touched this canvas. Those brushstrokes in the corner of this magnificent mural, those are mine. I was a part of this life, and it is a part of me." Marriage is to belong to each other through a unique and diverse collaboration, like two threads crossing in different directions, yet weaving one tapestry together.

The secret of love and marriage is similar to that of religion itself. It is the emergence of the larger self. It is the finding of one's life by losing it. Such is the privilege of husband and wife – to be each himself, herself and yet another; to face the world strong, with the courage of two.

To make this relationship work, therefore, takes more than love. It takes trust, to know in your hearts that you want only the best for each other. It takes dedication, to stay open to one another, to learn and grow, even when it is difficult to do so. And it takes faith, to go forward together without knowing what the future holds for both of you. While love is our natural state of being, these other qualities are not as easy to come by. They are not a destination, but a journey.

The true art of married life is in this inner spiritual journey. It is a mutual enrichment, a give and take between two personalities, a mingling of two endowments which diminishes neither, but enhances both.

Blessings

Though the following selections are printed here as blessings, and have been used as such in previous marriage ceremonies, you are welcome to use them wherever you find appropriate. They could be used as readings, during a ceremony, or even as toasts, at a reception. As you read through them you will find material that is appropriate for second marriages, renewal ceremonies and for naming ceremonies.

General

A Blessing

May the good Lord give you:
Enough happiness to keep you content,
Enough trials to keep you strong,
Enough sorrow to keep you human,
Enough hope to keep you happy,
Enough failure to keep you humble,
Enough success to keep you eager,
Enough friends to give you comfort,
Enough wealth to meet your needs,
Enough enthusiasm to look forward.
Enough faith to banish depression,
Enough determination to make each day better than yesterday,
And may we in turn thank you, O Lord, for your blessings.

(Author unknown)

May your joys be as deep as the ocean,
And your sorrows as light as its foam.

(Author unknown)

Weddings

Drink To Me

Ben Johnson

Drink to me only with thine eyes
And I will pledge with mine;
Or leave a kiss but in the cup,
And I'll not ask for wine.
The thirst that from the soul doth rise
Doth ask a drink divine,
But might I of Jove's nectar sup,
I would not change for thine.

May you need one another — but not out of weakness.

May you want one another — but not out of lack.

May you entice one another — but not compel.

May you embrace one another — but not encircle.

May you have happiness — and find it in making one another happy.

May you have love — and find it by loving one another.

May the passing of time serve to enhance the wonder of the journey on which you embark today.

(Author unknown)

Soul Mates

Jennifer M. Spencer

The quiet miracle
Of a man and woman
Uniting as one,
To travel the road of happy destiny
Together,
Is like a sacred haven in the sky,
The feeling of having arrived
Without ever leaving.

May you always need one another — not so much to fill your emptiness as to help you know your fullness.

A mountain needs a valley to be complete; the valley does not make the mountain less, but more; and the valley is more a valley because it has a mountain towering over it.

So let it be with you and you. (Author unknown)

May you succeed in all important ways with one another, and not fail in the little graces.

May you look for things to praise, often say, "I love you," and take no notice of small faults.

If you have quarrels that push you apart, may both of you have good sense enough to take the first step back. (Author unknown)

Second Marriage

Margaret Anne Huffman

We came late together,

O God of second chances,

Making the discovery of our love even sweeter.

We honor all that has brought us to this moment, trusting in
your promise to make all things new.

Give us many years to share

So that we can weave them together with vibrant strands of
loyalty,

Kindness, and warmth into a coverlet of married love, a
wedding gift from You.

In Support of Second Marriages

Were a man not to marry a second time, it might be concluded
that his first wife

Had given him a disgust for marriage; but by taking a second
wife he pays the highest compliment to the first.

(Samuel Johnson)

Children

Celebration on the Birth of a Child

Gertrude Hanson

We dare not carry it alone,

This sacred call to parenthood...

In humbleness we bow our heads to plead

For all the help that we shall need.

We pray for understanding hearts,

For courage, love, for songs to sing,

And staffs for paths that must be trod...

We are in partnership with God.

I love these little people; and it is not a slight thing when they, who are so fresh from God, love us.

(Charles Dickens)

A Christening Celebration Grace

Holy God, Creator of all life, bless _____, whom we have sprinkled today with the water of faith and love.

Thank you for all new life, for each new day, and for the support of family and friends.

Amen.

(Author Unknown)

Renewal

O God, we thank you, that you so directed our lives, that we found each other and together have been able to discover what it means to truly love.

Let us never take each other for granted.

Continue to teach us to be courteous in speech and act, to be sensitive to know how the other one feels, to take time to know what is important to the other and then help our loved one attain treasured goals.

To daily practise expressing appreciation, to share daily chores and family responsibilities, and to face all life bravely with united hearts.

Quicken within our hearts a fresh sense of romance and a spirit of praise and thanksgiving so that whatever spot on earth becomes our home, contentment, peace, harmony and joy will characterize it.

In Christ's name we ask. Amen.

(Author Unknown)

An Anniversary Toast

Let the purpose of all marriages
And friendships alike be
The deepening of the spirit
And the enrichment of the soul.

(Author Unknown)

For Our Anniversary

Mary Eastham

This much I know is true —
The secret to lasting love
Is in the details —
A hand to hold
When I'm feeling sad,
The circle of your arms
Around me
When the cold night air closes in.

I can tell you anything
And you won't laugh
Or run away.
Partners for life you and I,
We're marathoners
Who've learned to keep the pace
Straight and steady.

When I say the word "us"
I think of the day we met
And all the days in between,
That sense of place, of belonging
That begins and ends with you.

Milestone Anniversary

Margaret Anne Huffman

The couple we honor today speaks a language that's made a lifetime of commitment possible.

It is a thousand "I told you so's" swallowed in patience; a hundred "if you had's" silently forgiven, and dozens of daily "I love you's" never forgotten or taken lightly.

We, who can only eavesdrop around the edges of this ongoing conversation, hear between its lines a cherishing where these lovers, who are friends, laugh together at the end of rough days, cry together when needed, and awaken after all these years turned toward the other with still more to say.

They delight in new things yet to discover, surprises still to learn about their love for one another, new interests and directions to share — all leading to even more reasons they're glad to be married.

Continue to bless and inspire the writers of this rare one-of-a-kind tale.

What greater thing is there for two human souls than to feel that they are joined for life... to strengthen each other in all labour, to rest on each other in all sorrow, to minister to each other in all pain, to be one with each other in silent, unspeakable memories at the moment of the last parting.

(George Eliot)

Your
Wedding with Style

Money may not buy you love, but it surely does help you pay for all the details of getting married. So unless you are going to elope (and leave nothing but footprints), you'll need to do some planning to spend your money wisely. You may wish to put all your possible expenses into a personal order of importance.

The Photographer

If you want great photographs of your wedding, you will need to take care in selecting a photographer. It may sound trite, but you won't be doing retakes, so it makes sense to ensure that the person you choose can interact well with guests and do the job you want done. Don't make the mistake of confusing a person who owns a camera with a photographer. You will want plenty of pictures, and by all means encourage your friends and family to take as many as they can and to share them with you afterwards. Just remember that professional photographers are often asked if they can salvage amateur photos of a wedding because "these are the only ones we have."

Some couples choose to have their wedding videotaped. Choose your videotaper as carefully as you choose a photographer. Many of the same guidelines apply.

Word of mouth can be valuable in finding a suitable photographer. Wedding consultants may be able to suggest several. If you are searching through the Yellow Pages, look for professional designations — Alberta Association of Professional Photographers (APPA) and Professional Photographers of Canada (PPOC), or ask about accreditation when you call to set up an interview. Do set up an interview; if you hire over the phone you do not know what you are getting. Try to hire someone who does a lot of wedding photography and can show you samples of work that are in tune with the way you envision your own pictures.

Glossy black-and-white, hand-tinted work, sepia tones to give an old fashioned look, are all alternatives to colour work. The style of your wedding can influence the tone and level of formality you want your photographs to have. Be sure your prospective photographer knows your preferences and enjoys making the kind of pictures you want.

All professional photographers will have extensive portfolios and a variety of packages. Remember that when you hire a professional photographer you are buying his or her creative art and expect to pay accordingly.

Go to your interview prepared to ask a lot of questions, but don't be surprised to find an experienced photographer interviewing you. A good photographer will want to be very clear about your desires and expectations regarding your wedding photographs.

Use the questions below to guide you.

— How long have you been photographing weddings?

— Can I see photo samples of your previous weddings?

— Do you require a deposit to hold my booking?

— How long in advance do I have to make a firm booking?

— Do you offer special wedding packages? What do these include? Are you flexible; if I buy a package and then want some extra photos, how will these be priced?

— Is there a sitting fee included in these packages?

— Will you charge extra for travel to my site or is that included?

— Do I receive my negatives or do you hold these? for how long?

Professional photographers will have temperature-controlled storage systems for photographs, and while negatives fade over a long period of time, photos made from properly stored negatives will retain quality. It is a mistake to pay a photographer to take photographs and turn over film or negatives to you so that you can arrange your own processing or developing — the quality you will get at a one-hour service lab cannot begin to approach properly processed film and high quality developing from a lab that serves mainly professional photographers. An experienced wedding photographer should be able to explain the differences in greater detail if you are interested.

— Do you recommend any standard shots?

A good photographer will interview you in detail about your family and friends and about your preferences. Use sample albums that the photographer shows you to discuss this area further.

— If I wish, will you take pictures: at my home before the ceremony? during the ceremony? at the reception? of the receiving line?

Add any requests that are important to you and be sure to explain personal details about your friends and family if these need to be considered. For example, if some of your guests generally avoid each other, the photographer needs to know.

— What locations would you recommend for after-ceremony pictures?

If you have a location that you wish to use, let the photographer know and listen to the feedback you get about possible problems.

— How many pictures will you take?

— When can I expect my proofs to be available after the ceremony?

Planning the Wedding Reception

Most couples will choose to have some kind of reception or party to celebrate with their friends after the formal ceremony. Receptions can be long or short, held at any time of the day the couple choose, and include a large or small number of people. You can all sit down to have dinner followed by dancing, mingle over cocktails in an art gallery as your favourite musicians entertain, or enjoy a potluck picnic at the summit of a mountain peak.

There is no rule that says the reception comes right after the wedding. If a different arrangement suits you and your guests, feel free to wait — several hours, several days, it's your call. There are etiquette conventions that address "who pays for what" and books that will explain it all to you. However, more and more people are letting practicality, rather than tradition, make the "rules."

Generally, a reception held before noon tends to be informal and may feature a sit-down or buffet style brunch. Decorations and flowers are done with a light touch. A luncheon reception covers the noon-to-two time period. Hold your party mid-afternoon if you want to go really light, with tea and sandwiches with (or without) light desserts. If you met over ice-cream at the beach, nobody says you can't hold a ice-cream social. As a rule, as the hour of reception becomes later, the formality of the event often increases. This would be reflected in the decorations and flowers and the attire of the bridal party and guests.

If you hold the reception during the dinner hour, you need to plan a full meal. If you gather before dinner, cocktails would work well; after dinner gives you the flexibility of serving wine and cheese and/or dessert.

The resources section at the back of this book will give you some ideas. You can also talk to your friends, search the internet, or read the weddings, hotels, or restaurants sections of the telephone directory. Listen to each other when you plan your reception to be sure that it is right for you. If you want to have a large wedding, find a trusted friend or professional wedding planner to help make sure that you don't overlook important details. Many of the larger facilities (hotels, restaurants, golf clubs) may have a wedding consultant on their staff. If your gathering will be a small one, you can be less formal but it is still a good idea to enlist the help of a friend (perhaps a recently married one).

If you will have a lot of guests, we strongly advise that you set up a receiving line to greet them as they arrive. Brian Lee, author of *The Wedding M.C.*, summarizes the reasons very well in his book.

— All guests want to visit with the couple, to congratulate them and make them aware of their attendance.

— A receiving line saves time by reducing the amount of socializing during the reception.

— Many who attend the reception may not have been at the wedding ceremony and will not yet have greeted the couple.

— This is a "structured" opportunity for guests and relatives to meet the bridal party.

— It is a simple, yet valuable, way for guests who are quiet or shy to say "hello."

— It's fun too!

The Master (or Mistress) of Ceremonies

A master (or mistress) of ceremonies (MC) can be invaluable to the bride and groom if the reception is a large one. This person plays a key role: ensuring that transitions from mingling to eating to dancing are smooth ones, telling interesting or amusing stories about the couple and special guests, encouraging others who might have stories to tell or toasts to propose. Choosing an appropriate MC helps to ensure that everyone has a good time and that guests go home feeling much better acquainted. Brian Lee says that a great MC:

1. Has a positive attitude.

2. Plans the program carefully in close consultation with the families and participants. This includes the receiving line, head table sequence and introductions, the program sequencing and the dance.

3. Co-ordinates the involvement of organizers and volunteers.

4. Is an effective speaker committed to developing his/her personal speaking abilities through control of his/her content, delivery and audience.

5. Takes pride in his/her appearance and dresses for speaking success.

6. Does personal research for facts by getting to know the families and speakers.

7. Creates a great physical environment by overseeing the physical and technical set-up — leaving nothing to chance.

8. Co-ordinates the creation of an appropriate receiving line.

9. Performs the head-table introductions efficiently and humorously.

10. Shows sensitivity towards the program's speakers and the audience; he/she is particularly aware of timing.

11. Acknowledges all participants with enthusiasm.

12. May co-ordinate a dance program that is lively and entertaining.

13. Always has fun and projects a good sense of humour.

One of the best investments, in your own reception, that you can make, would be buying Brian's book for your selected MC.

Flowers

Flowers and weddings seem to go hand in hand. If you hire a planner, arranging for flowers is part of this person's responsibilities. Even if you have a relatively simple wedding, it is likely that you will at least carry a bouquet and that the groom will wear a flower in his lapel. Use the following as a checklist for flowers. You can write descriptions and quantities you will need for each category you choose to use.

Ceremony flowers for front of the room _____

_____

_____

Flowers for candle bases _____

_____

Flowers for guest-book table _____

_____

Boutonnieres _____

_____

Flowers for bride's hair _____

_____

Bouquet for bride _____

_____

Bouquets for attendants _____

_____

Flowers for flower girl _____

_____

Corsages for mothers, special guests _____

_____

_____

Table decorations _____

_____

Reception entrance decorations _____

_____

Bride's going-away corsage _____

_____

_____

Other _____

_____

_____

_____

There are many traditions that relate to flowers. We mentioned orange blossoms for the bride's headpiece in the chapter on rituals and myths, but a number of other flowers and herbs have been traditionally used for headpieces: rue (*Ruta graveolens*) by Lithuanian brides, rosemary (*Rosmarinus officinalis*) and bay (*Laurus nobilis*) in the seventeenth century.

Bridal bouquets, boutonnieres, and corsages often feature flowers used in symbolic ways. Sometimes the first letter of each flower name can be used to spell a wish or a name (Lavender, Orchid, Violet, Elder for LOVE). The Victorians developed a complex language of flowers which they employed not just at weddings, but to send a variety of messages between friends. You may enjoy the associations listed below and if you have an interest in further study please refer to the book by Geraldine Laufer listed in the **Resources** chapter. Other books may be available at your local library if you cannot find Geraldine's book.

Allium	unity, humility, patience
Bay laurel	success, personal achievement
Caraway	for prevention of infidelity
Clover	good luck, hard work

Comfrey	home sweet home
Forget-me-not	true love, remembrance
Johnny-jump-up	happy thoughts
Lamb's ears	support, softness, gentleness
Lavender	devotion, happiness, ardent attachment
Myrtle	marriage, love, fidelity, peace, joy
Nettle	cruelty, slander
Oregano	joy, happiness
Parsley	festivity, thanks, useful knowledge
Pinks	lively and pure affection, sweetness, newlyweds
Poppy	forgetfulness
Rosemary	remembrance, devotion, fidelity, wisdom
Sage	domestic virtue, wisdom, skill
Statice	never-ceasing remembrance
Thyme	activity, bravery, courage, strength
Violet	modesty, faithfulness, humility, simplicity, loyalty, "I return your love"

You may be intrigued to know that yellow roses are associated with infidelity. In any case, the world of flowers and herbs is a fascinating one.

Consider the possibilities in custom-made gift-giving, as well:
— herbal sachets for members of the bridal party — lacy ones for women
— masculine ones made of shirt fabric and decorated with buttons and a bow-tie for the men

— a lace pot-pourri stuffed teddy bear made for a flower girl
— herb and pot-pourri "dream-pillows" — all make lovely and inexpensive gifts.

The Wedding Cake

At any wedding reception, the bride's cake is probably the most familiar tradition. You can order any flavour of wedding cake you like, or layers of different flavours. Choose a reliable baker, preferably one who will allow you to sample several cakes and icings.

The size of the cake will depend upon the number of guests to be served. Professional bakers can give you reliable guidance. The cake is often placed on a separate, specially decorated table. Another excellent reason to have a professionally-made cake is that it will usually be delivered (in good condition) by someone who is used to doing just that.

If the cake is to be served as a main part of the refreshments, the bride and groom should cut it before the receiving line forms. If a large buffet or meal comes first, the cake usually remains uncut until a suitable time for dessert.

Bride and groom often cut the fist slice together. He might place his hand over hers on a decorated cake knife, and cut a slice from a lower, outer tier. Traditionally, each takes a bit of cake from the other's hand, and each offers the other a sip from a special toasting glass.

Another familiar tradition is that of the groom's cake. This is typically a dark cake, such as a fruitcake with marzipan icing. But again, choose whatever you wish, it's your party. The groom's cake (uncut), or the top tier of the bride's cake, may be saved for your first anniversary celebration. Pack and store the cake, in an airtight container, in a deep freeze (not the refrigerator freezing compartment) to prevent temperature changes which can affect the texture and flavour.

Usually, the groom's cake is distributed as a take-home favour for guests, with each piece placed in a small, decorated box provided by the baker. Even if you choose not to distribute cake in this way, you can participate in a delightful Italian custom, "bonbonnierie," and distribute candies packed in small boxes imprinted with your names and wedding date. Caterers or stationers can supply these boxes (and napkins, and match-books) if you wish. If you would rather thank your guests for attending in a more personal way, there are many possibilities: from small scrolls with inspirational inscriptions done in calligraphy to table decorations that can be dismantled and taken home. Browse through some books or magazines for ideas and put your imagination to work.

Saying Good-bye

There's no limit to how long you may enjoy your wedding reception. Guests may depart as they please, after the toasting and other scheduled formalities. If the reception location has been reserved for a limited time, the MC should see to it that guests know when to depart. Try to be available for farewells, or hand out favours to guests yourselves earlier.

You may change clothes before you leave the reception location if it is convenient. Planning a glamorous departure by limousine (or by horse and carriage) can be a classy way to avoid driving, after what is likely to have been a very full day. Do this and your worries about what guests might do to "decorate" your car disappear. Before you leave, be sure to talk with parents and other special guests, thanking them for their part in your day.

Finally, you can toss your bouquet and your garter and whisk away, followed by best wishes of your family and friends.

Attendants and Helpers

After you have decided on the style of your wedding, you'll be ready to select bride's attendants, groomsmen, and others who will be part of your ceremony. The formality of your wedding dictates approximate numbers of attendants.

Ultra formal — from 6 to 12 pairs

Formal — from 2 to 6 pairs

Semi-formal — from 1 to 2 pairs

Informal — none, or a pair of witnesses

Generally, one usher is needed for each fifty wedding guests. The number of other reception helpers varies.

Sisters, brothers, parents and close friends are all eligible to be selected as attendants. The bride usually selects her own attendants and the groom his. The numbers do not have to be equal. It is an honour to be invited, but there are associated responsibilities and expenses. Attendants usually pay for their own attire and transportation, buy gifts for the couple, and sometimes pay for and host parties or showers.

Responsibilities of Attendants

Usually, the **bride's honour attendant** (maid/matron of honour) will:

— purchase her own gown, shoes, hosiery and accessories, and arrange fittings.

— attend the rehearsal.

— plan and host a bridal shower (optional).

— assist the bride as requested, for example: addressing invitations, making phone calls, running errands.

— provide a dressing room emergency kit (safety pins, clear nail polish, needle and thread, comb/brush, and any other items that may be needed for last minute adjustments).

— confirm who will carry the groom's ring (if used) to the ceremony.

— provide special assistance during the ceremony (adjusting the bride's train, holding her bouquet, keeping the groom's ring until needed).

— mix with guests and create a congenial atmosphere at the reception.

Other bride's attendants (bridesmaids) will:

— purchase their own dresses, shoes, hosiery and accessories, and arrange necessary fittings.

— plan and host or help to plan and host a bridal shower (optional).

— attend the rehearsal.

— mix with guests at the reception.

The **groom's honour attendant** (best man) will usually:

— rent or provide his own attire and arrange fittings as needed.

— arrange and host a bachelor dinner or party (optional).

— attend the rehearsal.

— present the envelope containing payment for services to the marriage commissioner.

— transport the groom to the ceremony on time.

— carry the bride's ring (if used) until it is needed during the ceremony by the groom.

— help arrange transportation for the wedding party and honoured guests.

— propose the first wedding toast unless there is a designated master of ceremonies and help to provide a congenial atmosphere at the reception.

— protect the get-a-way car and luggage from pranksters.

— return the groom's wedding attire to the rental agency.

Other groom's attendants (groomsmen) will:

— rent/provide their own wedding attire and arrange fittings as needed.

— attend the rehearsal.

— mix with guests at the reception.

Usually the **head usher** will:

— rent/provide his own appropriate wedding attire and arrange fittings.

— attend the rehearsal and learn procedures for all activities connected with seating guests.

- keep a guest list and be sure special guests are appropriately seated.
- supervise other ushers.
- assist in organizing the processional.
- close the guest book at the proper time and seat latecomers unobtrusively (after the processional if need be).

Additional **ushers** will:
- rent/provide their own wedding attire and arrange fittings.
- attend the rehearsal.

Usually the **master (mistress) of ceremonies** (**MC**) will:
- rent/provide their own wedding attire and arrange fittings.
- prepare a speech to be given at the reception.
- prepare material for toasts which will be given during the reception.

Please see the previous section, **Your Wedding with Style**, for Brian Lee's valuable information about choosing an MC.

Large weddings may require a **photographer's assistant**. Usually a member of the family is designated to help, if a professional photographer has been hired. (The previous section, **Your Wedding with Style**, contains information about finding a wedding photographer.) The volunteer photographer's assistant will:
- assist the photographer as needed.
- identify important guests for the photographer.
- gather guests together for family and group portraits.

The **guest-book attendant** will:

— take charge of the guest book before the ceremony and during the reception and invite any guests who have not yet signed the guest book to do so.

— make sure the bride's mother (or bride) receives the book after the wedding.

The **cake attendant** will:

— learn to cut the wedding cake properly.

— cut the cake when directed by the bride or host.

If there are **other reception helpers** they will:

— assist as directed.

The bride may wish to invite children of friends or relatives to participate in the ceremony. Traditional roles include **flower girl**, **junior bridesmaid**, and **ring bearer**. Try to be sure that the children you choose will be co-operative and relatively calm under pressure. Select the child's parent or a friend to act as a coach ahead of time, and to guide the child through the ceremony on the day of the wedding.

Don't forget to include gifts for your attendants in the wedding budget. Consider jewelry, keepsake boxes, and desk accessories. These thank-you gifts need not be lavish, but should be thoughtfully selected.

Thank-you Notes

Traditionally, thank-you notes for wedding gifts are written on folded, good quality notepaper of a conservative colour. Thank-you notes should always be written as soon as possible after a gift is received. When gifts are received before the wedding occurs (and etiquette books do encourage invited guests to send their gifts ahead of time and discourage the custom of bringing gifts to the ceremony), it follows that the senders will also be thanked before the wedding. Notes, which the bride-to-be will write before the ceremony, are imprinted with her maiden name. After she is married, the married name, Mr. and Mrs. _____, is generally used on stationery.

Notes can be brief, but should always mention the specific gift, with compliments to the sender. Whoever writes the note – either the bride or groom – should mention the other partner.

Dear Mrs. Thompson,
Jill and I will enjoy using the elegant candlesticks in our new
    home. Thank you for your thoughtful gift and good wishes.
Sincerely,
                                    Jack

In acknowledging a gift of cash, do not mention the amount, but do mention a purchase that might be considered.

> Dear Aunt Liz,
>
> Your generous gift will very likely turn into the beautiful bedspread that has caught our fancy.
>
> Tom and I appreciate your kindness and look forward to seeing you at the wedding.
>
> With love,
>
> Sharon

If for any reason, a marriage does not take place, all gifts must be returned.

If an insured gift arrives broken, inform the sender immediately so that a claim can be filed. If a gift arrives broken or damaged from a local store, contact the store directly.

If a gift arrives with no identification of the giver, try to track down the source through the store. If that doesn't work, get the word out discreetly, among your friends. As a last resort, use or mention the gift during social occasions after you are married, and let your guests know that, "This lovely gift arrived, but we have been unable to determine who sent it."

Guests do often bring gifts to the wedding, despite the inconvenience that results. Be sure to have someone collect them and transport them to safekeeping after the wedding. Open these gifts and acknowledge them after the honeymoon.

Because weddings are public and often publicized events, in some communities it is advisable to hire security for the home, if a large number of valuable gifts will be unattended during the wedding and reception.

Above all, keep good records. An unacknowledged wedding gift is a serious social embarrassment.

If you receive gifts on the occasion of a christening or renewal, many of these same rules apply. You may not wish to go to the expense of buying printed thank-you notes, and it is quite acceptable to use plain stationery or notes purchased off the store shelf or created on your home computer and printer. The key is to remember to be prompt in thanking all those who have given you gifts.

Your helpers and attendants deserve special recognition. You can use the following as a worksheet, to ensure that you have not forgotten to thank any of your attendants.

Bride's honour attendant _____

Address & postal code _____

_____

Phone (____) _____

Thank you gift is _____

Notes _____

_____

_____

_____

_____

_____

_____

Bridesmaid _____

Address & postal code_____

_____

Phone (____) _____

Thank you gift is _____

Notes: _____

_____

_____

_____

_____

Bridesmaid _____

Address & postal code _____

_____

Phone (____) _____

Thank you gift is _____

Notes: _____

_____

_____

_____

_____

Groom's honour attendant _____

Address & postal code _____

_____

Phone (____) _____

Thank you gift is _____

Notes _____

_____

_____

_____

_____

Groomsman _____

Address & postal code _____

_____

Phone (____) _____

Thank you gift is _____

Notes _____

_____

_____

_____

_____

Groomsman _____

Address & postal code _____

_____

Phone (____) _____

Thank you gift is _____

Notes _____

_____

_____

_____

_____

Head usher _____

Address & postal code _____

_____

Phone (____) _____

Thank you gift is _____

Notes _____

_____

_____

_____

_____

Master/Mistress of ceremonies _____

Address & postal code _____

_____

Phone (_____) _____

Thank you gift is _____

Notes _____

_____

_____

Photographer _____

Address & postal code _____

_____

Phone (_____) _____

Fee for services _____

Volunteer photographer assistant _____

Address & postal code _____

_____

Phone (_____) _____

Thank you gift is _____

Notes _____

Guest book attendant _____

Address & postal code _____

Phone (_____) _____

Thank you gift is _____

Notes _____

_____

Cake attendant _____

Address & postal code _____

_____

Phone (_____) _____

Thank you gift is _____

Notes _____

_____

Marriage commissioner _____

Address & postal code _____

_____

Phone (_____) _____

Fee for services _____

Notes _____

Baby's Christening
Parents Ben & Michelle Schofield with Baby Ethan Bentley

*I love these little people; and it is not a slight thing
when they, who are so fresh from God, love us.*
(Charles Dickens)

Your Baby's Naming
or Christening Ceremony

A Christening or naming ceremony gives recognition to the significant event that has taken place through the arrival of a new son or daughter. Traditionally, this type of ceremony has been carried out in a church, or other house of worship, as a religious service. Today, much as some couples prefer secular marriage ceremonies, some families now prefer to make their own arrangements to mark this event as well. They view it as an opportunity to introduce the newest member of the family to members of the extended family and friends, and to formally name "Godparents" or "Mentors" for their child. It is a time to celebrate with the people who matter most to the new parents.

A civil Christening or naming ceremony is a non-religious ceremony. It is not a formal baptism like that conducted in many churches. However, if parents specifically request a prayer or religious reading, this can be included in a civil Christening or naming ceremony.

From the earliest times, humankind has used both religious and non-religious ceremonies to welcome the arrival of new children. Through ceremonies, we express feelings and emotions that we can never quite express in any other way, as we celebrate the most important events of our lives.

As part of the preparation for the naming ritual, parents usually select two people, whom they love and respect to be "mentors" or "godparents" for their child.

Sometimes those chosen are termed "godparents," sometimes they are called "mentors." It is up to you — the parents, which term you are most comfortable with.

It is most important that you discuss and agree about the responsibilities of godparents/mentors with the very special people you have chosen to fill these roles. Sometimes, these people are expected to become guardians for the children in the event that the parents are unable to fill that role (and this would also need to be formalized in a legal will). Sometimes, they are little more than close friends who would attend formal and informal family gatherings. Often the role to be filled falls somewhere between these two ends of the continuum.

Some definitions:

Godparents were originally the people who stood as sponsors for a child at his or her Baptism into the church. It is now used to mean those selected "significant others" — adults who promise to care about and help guide a child through life.

Mentor originally meant a wise and trusted counsellor. It has come to mean a particular person that one can look to for advice and guidance.

When you choose to have a civil naming or Christening ceremony, the marriage commissioner or other officiant, together with you, the child's parents, develops a ceremony to represent the style of spiritual life the child will honour until he/she reaches adulthood. In most cases this ceremony sets the stage for how the child will live his or her entire life.

Use the following as a suggested guide when planning your own formal naming.

Ceremony:

1. Welcoming of family and friends

2. Musical selection/soloist

3. Officiant addresses the gathering, receives the child from one of the parents, announces the name of the child to the gathering, and reads or invites another to read a verse in honour of the occasion

4. Presentation of gifts to the child

5. Obligations to the child are stated by the chosen godparents or mentors

6. Officiant gives the child to the mother, father, or mentor(s)

7. This person speaks to the gathering or gives a reading

8. Musical selection

9. Flowers or other gifts are given to the family

10. Blessing of all those present

11. Reception

This is an example of how a naming ceremony might be
conducted by a marriage commissioner or other person chosen
to officiate. We begin the example at step 3 to give you a view of
how the ceremony would unfold.

Officiant: *We are here today to celebrate a new life.
Historically, the ceremony of giving or taking on a new name
has always been an important occasion. We are here to
recognize that the importance of this ritual remains
undiminished today.*

*We give thanks for this young life and for the opportunity we
have been given to help nourish and guide that life. Both
parents and mentors have a role to play in this great
responsibility. Do not neglect your duty — children are our
promise of a better world.*

*They are like flowers — full of purity and grace. Flowers
enhance our appreciation of beauty.*

Children will grow and flower if we feed them with our love.

*We are grateful for the blessing endowed on
_____ and _____ through the
gift of this new life.*

*May this child help to draw out the best in you, as you grow
closer to each other in order to nurture **him/her**.*

*As this child grows in years may **he/she** also grow in strength
and wisdom, guided by your love and by the love of
_____ and _____, whom you
have chosen to be mentors.* (Officiant holds out hands to receive
the child.)

What name(s) do you give to this child? (Answer is given.)

I ask that these flowers (indicates flowers on table) *and all of you gathered here, bear witness to the beauty of the new life, which I hold in my hands. I give you the name your parents have chosen, and call you* _____.

As you travel through this life, _____, *may you find blessings and guidance, aid in times of trouble, comfort when you experience sorrow, inspiration in your quest for truth. Who will come forward to offer a reading to guide this child on life's journey?* (Reading can occur at this point.)

Would the mentors chosen for _____ *by those who love him/her most, his/her parents, please come forward.* (Mentors come forward. If they will give gifts to the child at this point, the officiant asks:) *Do you bring gifts for this child?* (They answer and gifts are placed on the table.) *Do you promise to guide and care for this child?* (This section can be as long as needed to detail the responsibilities of the mentors. Question and affirmation format is adaptable for this purpose. The officiant can ask the question, and mentors can respond *"We promise ...."* or more simply reply *"We do,"* in unison.)

You have made solemn promises to _____, *in recognition of this, I give him/her into your hands.* (Mentors reply, *"We thank you."* One, or both in turn, can speak or give a reading at this point.)

The ceremony can continue with music, followed by gifts and congratulations to the family from guests. The officiant can introduce each segment that the parents have chosen to include in the ceremony. Finally, the ceremony closes with a blessing of the child, parents, mentors and all those gathered for the occasion.

Officiant: *May all the blessings which this life can offer be upon _____, on his/her parents, mentors, and upon each one of us.*

It is your option, when you choose to have a civil ceremony to formally name your child, whether you invoke a deity, great spirit and/or spirit guides, or any other force which gives you comfort or strength. No direct references of this kind have been included in the example given, but they can easily be inserted where appropriate if the parents wish. Discuss your preferences with your selected officiant.

You should also consider having your marriage commissioner or other officiant, draw up or sign a certificate that you will keep, to commemorate the occasion. Samples are included in the back of this book and you can order certificates from the publisher. You will receive a quality 8 1/2 x 11 certificate, suitable for framing.

Renewal Couple
Mr. & Mrs. Bert & Heather Furseth

*The happiness of married life depends upon making small
sacrifices with readiness and cheerfulness.*
(John Selden—1534-1634)

The Renewal of Vows Ceremony

Through ceremonies we give voice to feelings and emotions that we can never quite express in any other way. Couples may decide to hold a ceremony to "renew their vows" for a number of different reasons. They may see this as a way to show that they still love each other, as a lovely way to celebrate their commitment to their marriage. Alternatively, they may have eloped or had only a very basic wedding the first time around, and view the planned reaffirmation of their vows as a way to indulge themselves in having "the works" with a second ceremony.

When you renew your vows, you are speaking, first of all, to each other and, second, to your family and friends, invited to share your special occasion.

Some couples choose to re-enact as closely as possible what happened on their original wedding day. This is the type of re-affirmation when you say, to each other:

"Everything that I said at our wedding, I mean in the same way today. I still love you and I wish to renew my promises made to you."

Some couples believe that the progress they have made within their relationship or the changes in their lives suggest a need to hold a renewal ceremony quite different from their wedding. They choose to make new promises that express more appropriately their relationship today. These couples are saying to each other:

"My love has matured and grown since our wedding day. I want you to know that my commitment to you is just as strong, and maybe stronger than it was, because of what we have shared together."

Having a renewal ceremony is a joint decision and can become a very meaningful occasion in your lives. You have a lot of flexibility in terms of where you hold your ceremony, who you invite to officiate and participate, what you wear, whether you exchange vows only or also gifts (rings and flowers are most commonly used), and what else occurs during the ceremony and afterwards.

It is important to choose a marriage commissioner who has the experience and the skills to create a ceremony based on your desires. This person should know how to take the words that you choose and add to them the symbolism and structure needed to create a meaningful and memorable ceremony.

A well-designed ceremony has a clear structure. It flows smoothly, maintains everyone's interest and remains personal and intimate throughout. The music and poetry should be designed to complement the ceremony. Your guests should feel your warmth and pleasure in each other, as they share this memorable event with you both.

Your Renewal of Vows Ceremony can be formal or relaxed, but its most important attribute is to express what the two of you want to say about your relationship.

Consider these suggestions:

1. Do both of you want a renewal ceremony? Talk together about what you would like to express to each other and to family and friends through your Renewal of Vows Ceremony. Having this discussion will increase the personal value of your ceremony.

2. Consider whether you want to repeat the same vows or have something very different. A marriage commissioner should be willing to suggest some alternative vows for you to use. You may wish to write your own based on your family's input.

3. Consider whether you want others to take part in the ceremony with you. Do you want to invite your original attendants or someone entirely different? Do you want children, grandchildren, other relatives or friends to participate?

4. How formal do you want to make this ceremony? Formal invitations, formal attire, fully scripted service complete with wedding party and ring exchange, full-scale reception with dinner and dancing fall at one end of the spectrum. The two of you and a few close friends, at home, on a beach or a mountain top, exchanging promises and toasting the occasion with champagne or passing the trail mix and drinking from your own water bottles would come at the other.

If the answer to the first (and most important) question from the previous section, "Do both of you want to have this ceremony?" is yes, then planning a renewal ceremony goes smoothly when you proceed by answering these questions. You may also wish to refer to the section on planning marriage ceremonies.

1. What do you wish to say to your family and friends about your life together as a married couple?

2. Will you use a variation of your original marriage ceremony or have entirely different vows? Make note of your preliminary thoughts, based on the answers to these two questions.

3. Do you desire to have this ceremony with your original wedding party and is it possible to do this? Would you rather have a ceremony where only your current family members play key roles?

4. Will you have a family meeting to discuss the ceremony and to invite opinions of family members regarding their participation? Will you plan everything or will you ask others to take part, or even to surprise you with their secretly-planned contribution to the occasion?

5. Will the date or time of the ceremony relate to your wedding date or time?

6. Will you exchange rings? You may use your original rings or new ones. You may wish to exchange some other gifts instead.

7. Do you want the lighting of candles to be part of your ceremony? You may wish to read the sections of this book relating to candle ceremonies to help you decide.

8. What level of formality do you want?

9. Who will you invite?

10. What arrangements need to be made based on the answers to the previous two questions (invitations, rented hall or other location)?

11. Do you want a marriage commissioner to lend expertise in planning and writing your ceremony? Do you want this person to be your master/mistress of ceremonies? You may wish to refer to the section of the book that deals with selecting a marriage commissioner.

12. Do you wish to have keepsakes of your renewal ceremony? Guest books, designated photographers, and commemorative certificates can all serve to preserve the occasion. Personalized copies of the sample certificate reproduced in the back of this book can be ordered from the publisher. You will receive a quality certificate printed on 8 1/2 x 11 paper, suitable for framing.

Use the following outline of the sequence of a formal renewal ceremony as a basis for planning your ceremony. Clearly, you would use only the portions that reflect your renewal ceremony plans. For each step in the sequence, you need to plan who will speak and then write out (as far as you wish to determine it) the script of what they will say.

Welcome of family and friends
Renewal vows (original or newly written)
Exchange of rings / Lighting of candles
Declaration of renewal (by master of ceremonies)
Blessing of couple
Special address(es) or entertainment by family or friends
Renewal affirmation and
greeting/congratulation of couple by guests
Reception

The next section includes some sample vows for your consideration. Following the above outline, these would be spoken by the couple, with the prompting of a marriage commissioner or other master of ceremonies, after the seating and greeting of all those invited to the renewal ceremony. Where contrasting type appears in the vows, substitute the appropriate wording.

My Oath to You

When you are sad, I will dry your tears.

When you are scared, I will comfort your fears.

When you are worried, I will give you hope.

When you are confused, I will help you cope.

And when you are lost, and can't see the light, I will be your beacon, shining ever so bright.

This is my oath, I pledge to the end.

Why, you may ask? – because you are my lover and friend.

I take you, _____, once again, as my **Husband/Wife**.

Once before, we said: "I do."

Through our __ years together, I have stood by your side and now, as we stand together, a married couple, may we continue to complement each other, and be exactly what each other needs, as our love and commitment become deeper still, throughout our lives together.

_____, I take you, once again as my **Husband/Wife**.

The word renaissance means rebirth.

Today, we celebrate the rebirth of our commitment before this honoured gathering.

_____, with full confidence, solidly anchored in our love, I take you this day, and for all the days, as my **Husband/Wife**.

I believe in this marriage more strongly than ever, _____.

It is with joy, born of experience and trust, that I commit myself once again to be your **Husband/Wife**.

Once before, I stood before family and friends and once again, I take your hand as my partner.

_____, I take you again as my **Husband/Wife**.

Perhaps the only thing truer than one's first love, is to recommit to that love before our family and friends.

_____, you were and are my love for life.

I take you from this day forward as my **Husband/Wife**.

As we continue to face our future together,
I promise to stand by your side.
With you by my side,
may we continue to complement each other
and be exactly what the other needs,
as our love and commitment continue to deepen
throughout our married life.
I take you, _____, once again as my **Husband/Wife**.

❦

Thank you for letting me love you, for ___ years of marriage.
Falling in love is wonderful, but staying in love is even better.
I am a better person because of you, and because of us.
_____, I take you once again
to be my **Husband/Wife**.

❦

I, _____,
take you, _____,
to be my **Husband/Wife**,
to laugh with you in joy,
to grieve with you in sorrow,
to grow with you in love,
wherever life may take us,
so that together, we may continue as partners
for the rest of our lives.

If rings will be part of your ceremony, a reading such as the following can be used next in the sequence. Fill in the blanks as needed.

Ring Service for a Renewal

Master of ceremonies: *A circle is the ancient symbol of wholeness and peace. It also represents the boundaries beyond which a relationship does not extend.*

In the form of a ring – the circle is the accepted token of a marriage covenant. As these rings are fashioned from one of the earth's most precious material, _____, so may your love, nourished and sustained by the love of God, be the most precious and durable of the values you share. In giving and receiving these rings, you again acknowledge that your lives remain joined in one unbroken circle.

Wherever you go, you will always return to your shared life together.

⚘

If you elect to use candles, you may wish to refer to this sample service.

Candle Lighting for a Renewal

Officiant: _____ *years ago, _____ and _____ joined their lives together in marriage and in doing so they combined their two separate lives into a new and living reality.*

Today, on the table there are three candles, which symbolize their individuality as well as their union.

_____ *and* _____ *will now light the*
outside taper candles which represent their individual lives.
Then with the flames of those candles, they will light the centre
candle which symbolizes their life together. We call that candle
the "Unity Candle."

May it burn brightly. May your lives be filled with many
blessings through all the years to come.

From this point, the ceremony would progress to readings or
other entertainment by family or friends.

The formalities would end with a pronouncement or a
presentation of the couple to the group, similar to that made at
the end of a wedding ceremony.

The assembled guests could then come forward to congratulate
the couple.

Resources

Books

Relationships

Whalen, Nomi, *Before We Say "I Do."* Detselig Enterprises, Calgary AB, 1999.
Excellent book for anyone interested in getting to know their partner better or exploring their relationship. Book ordering and other information is available on Nomi's website, www.weddingsbynomi.com.

Poetry and Vows

Ackerman, Diane and Jeanne MacKin (eds.), *The Book of Love.* Norton, 1998.
Anthology, includes passages from love letters.

Bryant, William Cullen (ed.), *The Library of World Poetry.* Grammercy, 1999.

Haas, Robert and Stephen Mitchell, *Into the Garden: A wedding anthology.* Harper Perennial, 1994.

Kingma, Daphne Rose, *Weddings from the Heart: Contemporary and traditional ceremonies for an unforgettable wedding.* Conari Press, 1995.

Munro, Eleanor (ed.), *Wedding Readings: Centuries of writing and rituals on love and marriage.* Penguin Books, 1996.

Stallworthy, John (ed.), *A Book of Love Poetry.* Oxford University Press, 1986.
Especially note the "Celebrations" chapter.

Warner, Diane, *Complete Book of Wedding Vows.* Career Press, 1996.
Contains traditional, non-traditional, and multi-cultural vows for couples from all walks of life.

Wedding Planning

Laufer, Geraldine A., *Tussie-Mussies: the Victorian art of expressing yourself.* Workman Press, 1993.
Informative guide to the symbolism of herbs and flowers.

Lee, Brian C., *The Wedding M. C.* Mastery Publishing Co., Calgary AB, 1998.
A step-by-step how-to guide to speaking at weddings for would-be MCs.

Long, Becky, *Something Old, Something New: 701 creative ways to personalize your wedding.* Meadowbrook Press, 1997.
Contains excellent section on multi-ethic wedding traditions.

Websites of Interest

A complete listing of Alberta Marriage Commissioners may be obtained from the Alberta government website: www3.gov.ab.ca/gs/information/vs/marriage/commissioner.cfm

Alberta Marriage Commissioner
Carollyne B. Rayner
Email: crayner@shaw.ca
Phone: (403) 283-4770
Website: www.craynerAlbertaMarriageCommissioner.com
Carollyne invites all brides and grooms to review her new book.

For most major communities in the province, try www.discovercommunity.com (substituting the name for "community" of course) or going to www.discoveralberta.com. For example, through www.discoverjasper.com, it is possible to link to virtually any wedding-related service or facility in the Jasper area.

Wedding Sites

The sites listed here are not meant to provide an exhaustive list. We invite readers to make suggestions for inclusion in the next edition of this book. We have not intentionally omitted any community or region of the province, rather we have written about what we know directly or through connections of various kinds. If you can supply information relating to Northern or Eastern areas of the province, for example, we urge you to correspond with the publisher. Again, please refer to the "discover Alberta" website for more complete coverage.

Calgary and area

Visit the website: www.discovercalgary.com for additional ideas.

Calgary Zoo
Calgary, Alberta
Events Co-ordinator
Phone: 403 232-9300

Canada Olympic Park
on the western edge of Calgary, Hwy 1
features a 90m ski-jump tower
Naturbahn Teahouse
Events Co-ordinator
Website: www.coda.ab.ca
Phone: 403 247-5465

The Conference Centre at Country Gardens
access via 17th Avenue S.W. then Lower Springbank Road
Blair Collins & James Tweddie, Centre Co-directors
Website: www.the-conference-centre.com
Phone: 403 242-5722

Devonian Gardens
in the heart of downtown Calgary
Top level (Level 4) Toronto Dominion Square
317 - 7th Avenue S.W.,
Calgary, Alberta
For information and booking contact
City of Calgary, Park Development & Operations
David Kroeker, Supervisor
Phone: 403 221-3782

Heritage Park Historical Village
1900 Heritage Drive S.W.
Calgary, Alberta
Events Co-ordinator
Phone: 403 268-8546

The Historic Deane House at Fort Calgary
806 - 9 Avenue S.E.
Calgary, Alberta
Robert Jensen — Dining room supervisor
Email: rjensen@fortcalgary.com
Website: www.fortcalgary.com
Phone: 403 269-7747

The Historical Cross House & Garden
1240 - 8 Avenue S.E.
Calgary, Alberta
Olivier Reynaud — Owner/Manager
Phone: 403 531-2767

The Wedding Pavillion
10817 West Valley Road S.W.
Calgary, Alberta
Liz Heitman — Vice-President & Wedding Planner
Website: www.weddingpavillion.com
Phone: 403 288-9558

Joining Hearts Studio & Candlelit Chapel
2830 Morley Trail N.W.
Calgary, Alberta
Corina Hill & Kathy McCabe — Wedding Planners
Email: kathy@joininghearts.com
Website: www.joininghearts.com
Phone: 403 290-0630

Edmonton and area

To obtain a more complete listing of wedding sites in and around the Edmonton area you may wish to visit the website: www.discoveredmonton.com

Indoor sites

Muttart Observatory
9626 96A Street
Edmonton, Alberta
Phone: 780 496-1403

Prince of Wales Armouries Heritage Centre
10440 108 Ave NW
Edmonton, Alberta
Phone: 780 496-8710

Outdoor Sites

Government of Alberta Legislature grounds
108 Street and 98 Avenue
Edmonton, Alberta

Devonian Botanic Garden
Located on Hwy 60,
north of Devon
Phone: 780 987-2496
Website: http://www.discoveredmonton.com/devonian/
weddings.html#Weddings

Jasper and area

Through www.discoverjasper.com you can discover additional sites. Click on "Wedding Planner" to access Parks Canada and other area resources and sites. The most popular locations for Jasper weddings are:

Pyramid Lake Island

Maligne Lookout (just before the Canyon)

Jasper Park Lodge
on the shores of Lac Beauvert,
Jasper, Alberta
Phone: 780 852-3301
Fax: 780 852-5107/2120
Toll Free: 1-800-441-1414 (Canada & USA)

Tekarra Lodge
on the cliff-top path
overlooking the meeting of the Athabasca and Miette Rivers
Jasper, Alberta
Phone: 780 852-3058
Fax: 780 852-4636
Toll Free: 1-888-404-4540

Becker's Chalets
on the cliff overlooking the Athabasca River
Jasper, Alberta
Phone: 780 852-3779
Fax: 780 852-7202

Jasper Wedding Services

Jasper Tourism & Commerce
PO Box 98
Jasper, AB T0E 1E0
Email: jaspercc@incentre.net
www.jaspercanadianrockies.com
Phone: 780 852-3858

Heads Up Salon for Men & Women
Specializing in Weddings
622 Connaught Square (has an elevator)
Jasper, Alberta
Phone: 780 852-4602

Elysian Florals, Antiques & Gifts
614C Connaught Drive
Jasper, Alberta
Debby O'Bryan-Mercer — Wedding Planner
Phone: 780 852-3230
www.floralsjasper.com
email: panache@incentre.net

Jasper Registries & Licensing
303 Pyramid Avenue
PO Box 2169
Jasper, AB T0E 1E0
Phone: 780 852-5994
Fax: 780 852-5972
E-mail: jasperreg@incentre.net

Lethbridge and area

To obtain more information, visit www.citylethbridge.ab.ca.

Parks

Agriculture Canada Research Station
BBQ and washroom facilities
5403 - 1st Avenue
Lethbridge, Alberta
Phone: 403 327-4561
E-mail: lethbridge@em.agr.ca

Elks Compound in Indian Battle Park
shelter and cooking facilities, free use of grounds
Lethbridge, Alberta (west side)

Henderson Park
McGrath and South Parkside Drive
Lethbridge, Alberta
Phone: 403 320-3020 or 3009

Nikka Yuko Japanese Gardens
open mid-May to mid-October
McGrath Drive and 8th Avenue South
Lethbridge, Alberta
Phone: 403 328-3511
Email: nyjg@japanesgarden.ab.ca

Waterton National Park
90 km from Lethbridge
Prince of Wales Hotel
Waterton, Alberta
www.Info@watertonpark.com

Red Deer and area:

Additional information is available from
www.city.red-deer.ab.ca/recreation/recreationindex.html

Heritage Ranch
Hwy 2 North,
25 Riverview Park
Red Deer, Alberta
Contact: Pat & Cal Fox
Phone: 403 347-7794 or 347-4977
Email: rafterjj@telusplanet.net

McIntosh Tea House
4631 - 50 Street
Red Deer, Alberta
Phone: 403 346-1622
Email: tmadole@telusplanet.net

McCullough House
Kerry Wood Nature Centre
6300 - 45 Avenue
Red Deer, Alberta
Phone: 403 346-2010

West of Calgary

If you are getting married in the mountains or at an outside venue, try to ensure that you have an indoor option, which you can use if the weather does not co-operate. Check out the websites at www.discovercanmore.com or www.discoverbanff.com for additional information.

Rafter Six Ranch Resort
Seebe, AB T0L 1X0
Events Co-ordinator
Phone: 1-800-267-2624

Kananaskis

Brewster's Kananaskis Guest Ranch
Phone: 403 265-7094 (Calgary number)

The following two Kananaskis hotels, have access to three picturesque viewpoints, along the Kananaskis River which are popular for wedding ceremonies.

Delta Lodge at Kananaskis
Kananaskis Village
Phone: 403 591-7711

Kananaskis Inn
Kananaskis Village
Phone: 403 591-7500

Canmore

Higashikawa Friendship (Riverside) Park
Canmore, Alberta
located north of Bridge Road, access via River Road

An area south of Bridge Road and on the east side of the Bow
River offers another popular spot for an outdoor ceremony.
There is no formal park here, and it may be less busy. Parking is
at the canoe-take-out area south of the bridge, walk along the
river path to the first open area beyond the aspen.

Canmore Seniors' Drop-In Centre
Canmore, Alberta
Phone: 403 678-2457

Canmore Nordic Centre
100 1988 Olympic Way
Canmore, Alberta
Phone: 403 678-2400

Several hotels located in Canmore have wedding facilities. There
are a number of golf courses with clubhouse facilities, suitable
for a ceremony and reception located in this picture perfect
mountain setting. Check the website at
www.discovercanmore.com for more information.

Banff

Lovely outdoor locations in and around Banff include:

- Bow Falls

- Hoodoos

- Gazebo in Central Park

The Banff Springs Hotel is well known as a popular wedding site
for indoor or outdoor ceremonies and formal wedding
receptions.

Banff has numerous hotels and restaurants available.
Contact the Banff/Lake Louise Tourism Bureau, 403 762-8421 or
403 762-0270 for more detailed information.

Lake Louise and beyond

Chateau Lake Louise
111 Lake Louise Dr.
Lake Louise, Alberta
Phone: 403 522-3511
Chateau Lake Louise is well known for its picturesque setting.
Couples wishing to get away from the crowds use the meadow to
the west of the Chateau.

Moraine Lake and Moraine Lake Lodge
Lake Louise, Alberta
Phone: 403 522-3733

Post Hotel
200 Pipestone Dr.
Lake Louise, Alberta
Phone: 403 522-3989

Emerald Lake Lodge
Emerald Lake, Alberta
Toll-free: 1-800-663-6336
Website: www.emeraldlakelodge.com

Num-ti-jah Lodge
Bow Lake, Icefields Parkway
Phone: 403 522-2167

Index

Certificate of Naming

_____
beloved child of

_____
and
_____

was named and so embarked on life's journey.
Witnessed by numerous friends and family,
but especially by

_____
(officiating)
and by

_____   _____
(Godparent)   and   (Godparent)

at _____ this _____ day of _____

Certificate of Naming

_____
beloved child of

_____
and
_____
was named and so embarked on life's journey.
Witnessed by numerous friends and family,
but especially by

_____
(officiating)
and by
_____
and
_____   _____
(Mentor)   (Mentor)

at _____ this _____ day of _____

Certificate of Renewal

This will certify that

_____

and

_____

renewed their marriage vows,
witnessed by numerous friends and family, and

_____

(officiating)

Together, we will continue on this marvellous adventure, our life

_____   *and*   _____

(spouse)   *(spouse)*

signed

_____ *this* _____ *day of* _____

at _____

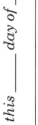

Books and certificates may be ordered from:

Turtle Publishing

Box 63124, 2604 Kensington Road N.W.

Calgary, Alberta T2N 4S5

On Canadian book orders, add **$7.00** per book and **$2.00** per certificate for shipping and handling.

On orders to be shipped outside of Canada, add **$10.00** per book and **$3.00** per certificate for shipping and handling.

Please call or e-mail **in advance** if you are ordering in quantity (8 or more books or certificates). You may qualify for a lower shipping/handling cost.

You Can Write "I Do"	Qty.	Price **$22.95**	Total
Renewal Certificate	Qty.	Price **$ 4.95**	Total
Naming Certificate Godparents	Qty.	Price **$ 4.95**	Total
Naming Certificate Mentors	Qty.	Price **$ 4.95**	Total

Ship to:	
Name _____	Merchandise total
Address_____	Add shipping cost
_____	Taxable subtotal
Phone _____	GST 7% (Canada only, except NF, NS, NB)
E-mail_____	HST 15% (in NF,NS,NB)
Fax _____	TOTAL

GST #873358113 RT0001

Cheques or money orders made out to Turtle Publishing must accompany order. No COD orders will be acccepted. Please do not mail cash.

Phone: (403) 283-4770 Fax: (403) 503-3356

Email: TurtlePublishing@shaw.ca

Website: www.craynerAlbertaMarriageCommissioner.com

Books and certificates may be ordered from:
Turtle Publishing
Box 63124, 2604 Kensington Road N.W.
Calgary, Alberta T2N 4S5

On Canadian book orders, add **$7.00** per book and **$2.00** per certificate for shipping and handling.

On orders to be shipped outside of Canada, add **$10.00** per book and **$3.00** per certificate for shipping and handling.

Please call or e-mail **in advance** if you are ordering in quantity (8 or more books or certificates). You may qualify for a lower shipping/handling cost.

You Can Write "I Do"	Qty.	Price **$22.95**	Total
Renewal Certificate	Qty.	Price **$ 4.95**	Total
Naming Certificate Godparents	Qty.	Price **$ 4.95**	Total
Naming Certificate Mentors	Qty.	Price **$ 4.95**	Total

Ship to:

Name _____

Address_____

_____

Phone _____

E-mail_____

Fax _____

Merchandise total	
Add shipping cost	
Taxable subtotal	
GST 7% (Canada only, except NF, NS, NB)	
HST 15% (in NF,NS,NB)	
TOTAL	

GST #873358113 RT0001

Cheques or money orders made out to Turtle Publishing must accompany order. No COD orders will be acccepted. Please do not mail cash.

Phone: (403) 283-4770 Fax: (403) 503-3356
Email: TurtlePublishing@shaw.ca
Website: www.craynerAlbertaMarriageCommissioner.com

Books and certificates may be ordered from:
Turtle Publishing
Box 63124, 2604 Kensington Road N.W.
Calgary, Alberta T2N 4S5

On Canadian book orders, add **$7.00** per book and **$2.00** per certificate for shipping and handling.

On orders to be shipped outside of Canada, add **$10.00** per book and **$3.00** per certificate for shipping and handling.

Please call or e-mail **in advance** if you are ordering in quantity (8 or more books or certificates). You may qualify for a lower shipping/handling cost.

You Can Write "I Do"	Qty.	Price **$22.95**	Total
Renewal Certificate	Qty.	Price **$ 4.95**	Total
Naming Certificate Godparents	Qty.	Price **$ 4.95**	Total
Naming Certificate Mentors	Qty.	Price **$ 4.95**	Total

Ship to:	
Name _____	Merchandise total
Address_____	Add shipping cost
_____	Taxable subtotal
Phone _____	GST 7% (Canada only, except NF, NS, NB)
E-mail_____	HST 15% (in NF,NS,NB)
Fax _____	TOTAL

GST #873358113 RT0001

Cheques or money orders made out to Turtle Publishing must accompany order. No COD orders will be acccepted. Please do not mail cash.

Phone: (403) 283-4770 Fax: (403) 503-3356
Email: TurtlePublishing@shaw.ca
Website: www.craynerAlbertaMarriageCommissioner.com

Life is a loving experience enjoyed by all creatures!

Carollyne B. Rayner